Studies in six 17th century writers

Ohio University Press
ATHENS, OHIO

Studies in six 17th century writers

JAMES ROY KING

To the late

JOHN C. WENTZ

chè in la mente m' è fitta, ed or mi accora,
  la cara e buona imagine paterna
  di voi . . .

Acknowledgements

For permission to quote, I wish to thank the following publishers: The Beacon Press, for passages from Sorokin, FORMS AND TECHNIQUES OF ALTRUISTIC AND SPIRITUAL GROWTH (1954); George Braziller, Inc., for passages from Murray, MYTH AND MYTHMAKING (1960); Columbia University Press, for a passage from Haller, THE RISE OF PURITANISM (1938); Doubleday and Company, for passages from Sypher, FOUR STAGES OF RENAISSANCE STYLE (1955), and from Harold G. Henderson, INTRODUCTION TO HAIKU (1958); E. P. Dutton and Company, for passages from Dante, THE DIVINE COMEDY (The Temple Classics); Harcourt, Brace and World, for a passage from C. S. Lewis, TILL WE HAVE FACES (1956); The Hutchinson Publishing Group, for passages from ZEN BUDDHISM: SELECTED WRITINGS OF D. T. SUZUKI; the Macmillan Company, for passages from Whitehead,

SCIENCE AND THE MODERN WORLD (1926) and MODES OF THOUGHT (1938); University of Minnesota Press, for passages from Dunn, SIR THOMAS BROWNE (1950); The Odyssey Press, for passages from TRISTRAM SHANDY, ed. Work (1940), and JOHN MILTON: COMPLETE POEMS AND MAJOR PROSE, ed. Hughes (1957); The Open Court Publishing Company, for a passage from Dewey, EXPERIENCE AND NATURE (1929); The Clarendon Press, Oxford, for passages from C. S. Lewis, PREFACE TO PARADISE LOST (1942), THE DIARY OF JOHN EVELYN, ed. DeBeer (1955), and THE WORKS OF HENRY VAUGHAN, 2nd edition, ed. Martin (1957); Random House, for a passage from Watts, THE WAY OF ZEN (1957); Rutgers University Press, for passages from JOSEPH HALL: HEAVEN UPON EARTH AND CHARACTERS OF VERTUES AND VICES, ed. Kirk (1948), and Brée, CAMUS (1959); Charles E. Tuttle Co., Inc., for a passage from Reps, ZEN FLESH, ZEN BONES (1957); Washington University Press, for a passage from SPRAT'S HISTORY OF THE ROYAL SOCIETY, ed. Cope and Jones (1958).

Contents

Preface

Biography is perhaps the most universally popular of literary forms. Part of its fascination lies, quite clearly, in the inspiration which the lives of great men provide, but a good deal of interest accrues, too, from the infinite variety of approaches possible to even the simplest and quietest human life. In our century biography has been written by Freudians interested in their own characteristic abstractions and by muckrakers with their luridly detailed pictures of degeneracy. Seventeenth-century biography, too, runs the gamut from the pious ejaculations about holy men which are the stock-in-trade of funeral sermons to the almost ludicrously trivial comments of John Aubrey—that Sir John Popham lived like a hog, that Ralph

Kettle dragged one foot, that Harvey regarded men as "great mischievous baboons," and that Thomas Hobbes was annoyed by flies on his bald head.

It is certainly possible to discuss human experience at a more sophisticated level: even in the 17th century, biographers like Bacon and Walton were concerning themselves with life-patterns and what Gordon Allport has called "broad intentional dispositions." This book undertakes to examine and evaluate certain patterns in the lives of six 17th century men of letters: the scope they chose to give their lives, the events that they made meaningful, the threats to integrity which they faced. Thinking about the experience of living is not a particularly popular activity today, and modern readers are frequently puzzled or confused when they encounter for the first time the idea of the "planned life" which is so important a part of Renaissance moral philosophy. Some are repelled by the traditional piety implied by titles like "Holy Living" or "The Plaine Mans Path-way to Heaven." Others are convinced that a man is better off if he faces life spontaneously, improvising as he moves from moment to moment, preserving always his freedom to respond to the unexpected. "What is your life like?" is thus a question that may elicit from sophisticated young people expressions of amazement or half-mocking disgust, and it will tie the tongues of those who should be capable of an objective and balanced analysis. This is unfortunate, since some valuable general truths are to be found in thinking about the structure of experience—insights into the problems of self-transcendence, ambiguity, commitment, scope, power, and meaning—as well as an enlarged understanding of certain books that have grown out of these problems.

All the great social and cultural crosscurrents of the 17th century left their mark upon the way men of this age organized their lives. Technological change, for example, encouraged in certain men a spirit of confidence and mastery; it forced some into narrow fields where they developed great skill; it impelled others to acquire broad knowledge in many areas. From some it drew a lifelong dedication; others it turned into brilliant dilettantes. It leveled great new challenges against human well-being. It permitted some to see the world almost as if it were alive; it tempted a few to pillage the world as a lifeless *thing*. Civil war at mid-century contributed to the success of a few men; it left many permanently scarred by shock or bitterness. It introduced a less rigorous control of men and thought, and it uncovered new leaders with new kinds of power. Still other responses were called up by the burgeoning of knowledge and speculative thought in the 17th century: old syntheses had to be reconstructed; men who in their younger days had entered holy orders found themselves preoccupied with mathematics or medicine; students of the classics found themselves challenged by students of the natural world who made lavish promises of material progress; the arena of human life was constantly being expanded by discoveries in geography, astronomy, and physiology; and freedom of thought became a lively issue. Some of those who found religion the central fact of life were beginning to regard the chief points of their faith as essentially symbolic or to stress the contribution that a spirit of love might make to human well-being. Others continued to see theology as an accurate, never-changing map of the divine world. Anglicanism and the dissenting sects produced sharply distinct character-types, and such diverse fields as politics, psychology, and physical science impinged as never before on religious faith. And where there appears a figure of Milton's intensity, all these broad issues intersect with problems that are more personal— the choice of a career, the nurturing of one's own personality, the experience of frustration and failure, avenues of self-transcendence, and the threat of death. A life-structure, like a novel or a cathedral, must be judged not only by its overall plan but also by the richness and refinement of its details and by the harmony of its materials with its inner design.

The kind of material I am concerned with in this book may prove valuable, I am hopeful, as an essential dimension for "the study of lives," a dimension that will complement and enlarge the meaning of details about heredity, environment, beliefs, and accomplishments. Questions of the kind I have posed often take us deep into a man's basic motivations without the dangers so often attendant upon amateur—or professional—psychoanalysis. Moreover, the structure we are discussing is a kind of evolving and developing constant which determines what a man sees or neglects and which gives a certain unity to themes and images from entirely different parts of his career. Then again, insight into the way a man structures his life may help us to identify the kind of power that belonged to him, how he came by it, and how he applied it.

In 1674 Nathaniel Fairfax observed, " 'Tis a more ticklish thing to pen a preface, than to write a book." Evidently he sensed the dangers that lie on every hand—of promising more than one can deliver, of assuming that one's ideas are more original than they really are, of insulting a reader with the obvious, puzzling him with private musings, or repelling him with "sheer ignorance." But since the delightful 17th century practice of long titles has been abandoned, there is no choice but to use a preface to tell the reader whether he has opened a book on Shang bronzes or chess end-games—and to provide him with some hint as to whether the author will prove a congenial companion or an insufferable bore. I want to use the preface, too, as a way of thanking for their patient and helpful criticism Professor M. A. Shaaber of the University of Pennsylvania, and Professor Malcolm Ross of the University of Toronto. Neither will be held responsible for my errors of fact or judgment, or for the idea of a book on this subject in the first place. I am also grateful to the staff of the Newberry Library, Chicago, for assistance; to colleagues and students at Wittenberg College, who on more than one occasion were my captive audience; and to the Rutgers University Research Council and to the Board of College Education and Church Vocations of the Lutheran Church in America for financial aid.

Studies in six 17th century writers

John Evelyn and the new world of technology 1

For three centuries John Evelyn has been loved and re-
spected by readers who have seen in him qualities which his
more brilliant friend, Samuel Pepys, did not possess. During
his lifetime Evelyn published well over a dozen volumes, on
subjects ranging from forestry to engraving, and his diary
covers the entire eighty-six years of his life, sometimes in
the very richest detail. A man of charm and some material
abundance, he maintained friendships with many of the
great figures of the 17th century. Yet for all his talent and
wide-ranging interests, Evelyn has frequently left his readers
wishing that he had been something more than he was. What
he did with his life and his world is not precisely what we

wish he had done. He seems to have been insulated from the deepest pleasures of travel, art, and friendship by serious personal deficiencies—a lack of warmth, pride in his social position, dullness of perception. He seems to have neglected his own inner being, succumbing to the more obvious features of the teeming life all around him; he was interested in too many things to master any. A kind of graying, twilight ghost of *l'uomo universale,* he confronted swirling currents of social change which he did not understand well enough to join and which he had little mind to fight. The potentially fruitful element of inner conflict which exists in every thoughtful man is in Evelyn too often reduced to getting his own way, and he seems to have been unaware of the ambiguities inherent in every position he took. A lover of gardens and a sympathetic friend, he nevertheless contributed to the dehumanization of the 17th century world and to a developing psychology of mastery and domination. His response to the 17th century scene is thus a complex and often contradictory product of opposing forces quite obviously puzzling to Evelyn and sometimes to his readers as well.

In 1667, answering a challenge from Sir George Mackenzie, Evelyn wrote the lively essay, *Public Employment and an Active Life . . . Preferred to Solitude.* Modern readers have found it one of the most characteristic and honest books he ever wrote. In essence, Evelyn's argument is that "men of parts" ought to use their talents in the service of society. He describes those who prefer solitary retreats as conjurors raising "a thousand melancholy devils" to endanger their generation, and he suggests, with an unbecoming sneer, that scholars who pore over their books while their families starve are improving the lot of no one. Retired

people, he observes, are victimized by all sorts of follies: one
man hunts for medals, another buys rusty iron kettles at
tinkers' shops, still others sit at cards, smoking, drinking,
revelling "without a grain of sense from dinner to midnight." [1] The problems raised by this essay are as old as those
of the city mouse and the country mouse, but the debate of
Evelyn and Mackenzie indicates that new and immensely
important issues were at stake. The medieval garden-city,
with open country just beyond its walls, had enabled men
to enjoy the best of both worlds. But at the beginning of modern times the European city expanded into the
fields, and the growing excitement of urban life made the
increasing isolation of the country more desirable—or completely intolerable.[2] In what he said to Mackenzie, Evelyn
reveals how deep within him lay the conflict of elemental
longings with practical considerations: the family home at
Wotton and his own house and garden, Sayes Court, pull
one way; the bustling activity at Whitehall pulls the other.
That Evelyn should have chosen the latter is no more than
might be expected from a man so fascinated by the vital
changes occurring in his age. That he turned his back on the
country is surprising, however, for elsewhere he describes
himself as "wood-born"; he wrote beautifully about gardens;
he boasted that he sucked in affection for solitude with his
mother's milk; and at the end of his life he welcomed eagerly
the peace of Wotton. What is more, Evelyn published this
essay in February, 1667, after a hectic year of urban life that
had involved him in both the plague and the fire. To express
an eagerness for further activity—as Evelyn does—suggests
either an incredible resistance to vicissitude or, less hero-
ically, a desire to be of continuing assistance to the great, a

need for more patronage money. I am less convinced than many readers of the essay's honesty; I find it, however, an absolutely typical expression of the unresolved ambiguities which haunted Evelyn at every stage of his life.

Throughout his career Evelyn faced choices like this one he tosses off so lightly in the essay to Mackenzie. Inevitably the dilemma rings some variant on the city-country theme: agricultural interests are pitted against technological; the contemplative life struggles with the active; instinctual powers war with the rational. The issue is not that Evelyn usually sides with new ways, despite a deep-seated leaning toward the old, but that he made the exclusive choices, too rarely using his considerable powers to illumine, soften, or humanize what was coming by what had been. It is not without significance that he lacked a philosophy of Nature. He was not without some speculative bent, for he translated Lucretius and sought the ethical counsel of Taylor. What is more, he thought long and effectively about the benefits England stood to gain from her natural resources. But the crucial problem of his age, the issue of cultural and technological revolution, he never faced. Childhood affections preserved to adulthood might have borne eloquent witness to certain human needs, but these affections were unsustained by any firm intellectual structure and so they were sacrificed constantly to the demands of the passing moment. Bacon's program for the advancement of science was firmly based on convictions about the fullness with which Nature conferred her blessings on man, a sense of the vital forces lodged in the natural world, a frank admission of the involvement of man in his environment, and a persistent turning from the study of final causes to examination of the ways Nature could serve mankind. Browne's peculiar blend of mysticism was sustained by a comprehension of Nature as "the art of God," and his sense of plenitude by a fundamentally scientific understanding of the process of generation. And Cudworth's Christian Platonism found its support—and its eloquent answer to Hobbes—in a conception of the plastic power of Nature through or by which the intelligence of the Creator operated. But of all such intellectual sustenance Evelyn was stripped. From the Diary we catch his wide-eyed admiration for the experiments he saw at meetings of the Royal Society, but we see also that he failed to grasp the significance of all this curious probing into the "bowels" of Nature. What Evelyn understood was the beauty and the superficial utility of the environment; what he enjoyed was manipulating it for his immediate profit and delight. This is certainly not surprising, for his century produced the greatest crop of literate gardeners England has ever known. Whatever repose Evelyn enjoyed, whatever contemporary reputation he achieved, and not a little of his usefulness to the great can be traced to his practical view of things. When the Royal Society sought permission to hang his picture in its hall, he objected, describing himself as "a planter of colewort." [3] But if there was any depth or wholeness in the man, it lay here in his warm love for green growing things.

I

There is no better way to capture the wonderful enthusiasm of this man for Nature—and all the deficiencies of his position—than to examine in detail some of his responses. Such a description should embrace Evelyn's comments on the gardens he visited, an estimate of his taste in horticulture

and his knowledge of the subject, an account of his books on
gardening, and an examination of his concern with England's
natural resources.

Those parts of the Diary which cover travel on the Continent are punctuated with enthusiastic comments on natural
beauty. It is significant that while Evelyn borrowed many
of his comments on cities and buildings from travel books
and newspapers, what he had to say about nature is usually
his own.[4] He traveled in a strangely assorted set of capacities—gardening expert, amateur soldier, social critic, student
of affairs, art expert, and rustic shepherd *à la* Watteau, enjoying, delighted, informed, but essentially untouched and
unchanged. Often we find him nearly helpless with delight
before some wild, grotesque, or otherwise romantic bit of
scenery. Sometimes the melancholy of evening touches him,
sometimes the sweetness of an Italian morning; the source
of delight may be a Belgian castle covered with ivy, or the
gardens of Justinian flooded with the song of nightingales.
At one moment he singles out as "horrid & solitary" a forest
between Paris and Fontainebleau (II, 116), and his description of the Simplon Pass bespeaks real terror: "Next morning we mount againe through strange, horrid & firefull
Craggs & tracts abounding in Pine trees, & onely inhabited
with Beares, Wolves, & *Wild Goates*. . . . Some of these
vast mountaines were but one intire stone, 'twixt whose clefts
now & then precipitated greate Cataracts of Mealted Snow"
(II, 509). The tone softens as Evelyn describes the quieter
beauty of walnut trees in Holland, vast cork forests near
Pisa, a hill of yews looking like "some new or enchanted
country," or the "one intire Orchard" which comprises
Herefordshire.[5] Nature writing turns quaint when he advises

that there is no need to break open the seed pods of pine and fir: *"Nature* does *obstetricate,"* or when he suggests that plants "beginning now to peep should be *earthed up,* and comforted a little." [6] But beyond the occasional flash of gratitude at some sweet morning or the pleasant moral observation that life in the woods destroys all dogmatism and self-assertiveness, Evelyn's tourist's eyes do not penetrate. No angels lurked behind the bushes in the gardens he visited; no comprehension develops of the subtle interplay between the life of man and the great rhythms of forest or farm, sea or mountains.

On January 17, 1653, by the light of a new moon, with a west wind blowing, Evelyn began to set out a great garden of his own on one hundred acres at Sayes Court, just east of London.[7] In the first half of the 17th Century, striking progress in agriculture had been made: new products like turnips and clover were introduced, new tools for plowing and sowing were invented, a threshing machine was developed, wastelands were drained and cultivated, fine breeds of cattle were being bred, and the knowledge of husbandry had been broadened. Technology was eliminating the element of inspiration from horticulture, transforming it into an art requiring both skill and knowledge. Much of what Evelyn knew had, of course, been acquired slowly in the gardens of the Luxembourg Palace, at the Tuileries, the Borghese Gardens, and in the smaller gardens of his English friends. Evelyn had learned about the effects to be achieved with a wide variety of fruit and shade trees, and in the gardens he planned he insisted that rare species be mixed with more common varieties. He liked to see some trees planted in careful rows, but others set out in groves, so that a portion of every garden was wilderness. Fruit trees trained on espaliers, romantic gardenhouses, trees twisted together, and "shady walkes in the box-coppses" (III, 157)—all these were sources of delight. He was impressed by fountains in the Borghese Gardens which sprayed water out in various shapes and by a pair that resembled musketeers shooting water out of their guns. Evelyn recommends the construction of gardens on more than one level, with cascades or marble-railed stairs to mark out the breaks in elevations. Like his contemporaries, he admired views or "prospects," and where limitations of space (as in a city) made the real thing impossible, he approved the practice of painting a vista on the garden wall. In one Parisian garden he saw a painting of the Arch of Constantine, life size, and so real that birds tried to fly through it. Where space made such "agreeable cheats" unnecessary, these vistas were to be produced by rows of trees radiating from a central axis, each avenue punctuated by fountains. The walks pictured in old prints are very long indeed, and Evelyn's enthusiasm grows accordingly.[8]

Evelyn shared the admiration of many of his contemporaries for parterres, those elaborate patterns of colored stones, sand, and flowers laid out on the grounds around great houses, frequently in the shape of endless knots. Some were large enough to contain bronze fountains; others were surrounded by boxwood hedges. Evelyn recommends a variety of arrangements of ponds and streams, as well as such miscellaneous attractions as the vivarium or zoo. From his descriptions it is evident that both the formal garden and the landscape garden were the 17th century aristocratic equivalent of the modern boardwalk fun house, the children's Christmas garden, or any such display designed to titillate

the eye, stir the most superficial emotions, arouse awe at the
financial outlay, and excite the fancy. I doubt that Evelyn's
response ever disappointed the well-heeled gardeners who
were his hosts and sought his approval.

But for all the childlike joy he took in display, he succeeded in becoming an authority whose advice was eagerly
sought by those whose money made possible such horticul-
tural magnificence. After the success of his own garden (its
evergreens and neatness were especially admired), he was
asked to lay out a garden at Albury, in Surrey, and he had
the satisfaction of seeing his plans carried out. At one time
or another he visited and gave opinions on the garden of
Lord Chancellor Arlington, Sir Josiah Childe (who spent
prodigiously on walnut trees and fish ponds "as suddainly
monied men" often do—IV, 306), of Lord Godolphin, and of
the Earl of Essex, who lavished vast sums on soil that was
"stonie, churlish & uneven" (IV, 200). It is hard not to share
with Evelyn the delight he took as he watched a cook at
Swallowfield fish carp out of the manor pond for dinner.

Evelyn's knowledge of the more practical parts of horticulture is displayed in *Sylva* (1664), the book which made
his reputation in the 17th century, the first book published
by the Royal Society. It reveals impressive mastery of technical data about trees, and it suggests the enthusiasm which
wood thoughts stirred in the heart of at least one advocate
of technological advance. Evelyn introduces his subject by
describing methods of getting trees by sowing seed or trans-
planting. He continues with a detailed discussion of the ad-
vantages, uses, and special problems associated with all the
important species. The oak, so highly esteemed by the Romans, comes first. Evelyn is interested in problems of mov-

ing such trees in their maturity, and he has heard of one estate owner who moved six hundred of them, eighty years old. The elm is described as fast growing, and doubts are cast on the statement of Salmasius that this tree will grow from scattered chips. (Nevertheless, says Evelyn, he will not dogmatize or speak "magisterially.") The beech is declared excellent for wooden bowls, dishes, and other products of the lathe; chestnuts are given to swine in England, whereas on the Continent they are regarded as "a lusty, and masculine food for *Rustics* at all times" (p. 25). Evelyn has a number of tricks to hasten the growth of the maple, expresses dislike for the sycamore, which covers walks with the glue from its leaves, and notes that birch wine neither dissolves gallstones nor makes a very sweet drink. He is amazed at the variety of climates in which the cedar will grow, from the Barbados to lands "where the *Snow* lyes . . . almost half the year" (p. 61), and he supplies information about fence making and hedge planting, about the pruning and felling of trees, about the seasoning of timber and manufacture of charcoal, and, in a supplement, about the making of cider. From the delightfully aromatic balsam, through the ash, walnut, lime, hazel, poplar, and pine, to the virtually incombustible larch —domestic and exotic trees, practical considerations and aesthetic—Evelyn's range of knowledge and interest is as impressive and appealing as it is comprehensive. Statistics which he supplies about timber sizes are amazing even in our day of superheroic figures and reveal the relevance of *Sylva* to problems of English national defense: Evelyn has seen beams of larch 120 feet long, masts ninety-nine feet high and nearly three feet in diameter, and a solid square beam forty feet long and three feet square. Through this man's world, where dilettantism is at least for the moment laid aside, Evelyn advances boldly, emerging eventually and in triumph "out of the *Wood*." [9]

Evelyn's response to trees and wood has to be seen as mythic or elemental. Trees provided for him the same kind of contact with basic substance that Michelangelo found in stone. Our hearts are stirred today whenever we hear about the great wooden houses of Norway, the wooden temples of Asia, by the fairy lore of the Black Forest, by wooden boats, old furniture, and the smell of lumber, by shavings curling from the blade of a plane, by the beauty of highly polished wood, and the equal beauty of wood rough hewn. Perhaps woodsmen cannot be expected to lead cultural revolutions; the trees which they tend are a prime symbol of the stable and the unchanging. Thus the love of men for forests is a fact of considerable comfort to those who worry about the madness of the world.

Evelyn's response to trees was not, of course, purely emotional, but it certainly was not confined to detailed, technical matters. It led him to a genuine understanding of the significance of England's natural resources—into areas known today as agricultural economics and ecology. The depths of his insights here provide an important gauge of his comprehension of the vast cultural revolution that was going forward in his age. His feelings are embodied in a comment in *Sylva* about the trees that "grace our Dwellings and protect our nation," and, like so many enthusiasts, he prophesied almost universal benefits from the nationwide program of tree planting which he advocated. He condemns bitterly the ruthless way the Puritans cut down England's "wooden walls," and he notes that in 1588 the Spanish Armada sailed to England with instructions to weaken England permanently by felling the forest of Dean. Parliament, thinks Evelyn, should order trees planted on all pieces of vacant land, encourage the planting of hedgerows, and prohibit the destruction of certain species. He suggests importing exotic varieties like the peach, plum, fig, and pear, as well as encouraging the fir and pine, which were so enriching the Scandinavians with their resinous by-products. His persistent appeal to the English apple growers—"give me good cider"—is a measure of his scorn for imported wine, and it provides a patriotic as well as economic shading to his enthusiasm for trees. All in all, Evelyn is a highly literate publicist for an arboreal economy, with an emotional involvement in the measures he advocates that goes back to his childhood and his rural patriotism.

II

Evelyn's proposals to Parliament have a certain timeless validity. When he made them, they were unusually relevant but also increasingly impractical. For by the 1660's such massive cultural and technological changes were getting under way that no program could have been comprehensive enough to embrace them. Indeed, as Walter Lippmann has observed, the chief mark of the industrial society which was being born was the very large scale on which it was organized and the very dynamic way in which it functioned. One of the primary symbols in Evelyn's work of these great changes is *coal,* a substance with cultural implications which have been very fully described by Professor Nef. It would, of course, be erroneous to attribute the smoke nuisance, about which Evelyn wrote *Fumifugium* (1661), to the Industrial Revolution, since coal did not come to be used in great quantities until the 19th century. (At the beginning of the 18th century water was the principal source of power for the textile industry.) The coal about which Evelyn complains had been used in London for four centuries, and frequent attempts to prohibit or control its use as a fuel had been made. Nevertheless, coal had increased in popularity during the 16th century, when the invention of cheap bricks made inexpensive chimneys possible, and as the population increased so did the severity of the problem.[10]

But it was not coal smoke alone that reflected technological advance. A great industrial expansion was taking place on land reclaimed from the Thames east of Wapping. Brett-James notes that parishioners in Stepney gave their occupations as mariners, sailors, shipfitters, anchorsmiths, coal merchants, chandlers, carpenters, rope makers, and sugar merchants.[11] At Blackwall the East India Company had its great docks for the building and repair of ships, heavy investments were being made in the 1670's in buildings for textile manufacturing, and the lime-burning and alum industries produced particularly noxious smells. Alum is made by boiling urine, and the smell is said to be dreadful: an alum plant was built in London in 1626, and for over three years its owners were able to disregard the orders of London authorities to move. Once even tentatively established, the factories proved almost impossible to eliminate. Yet Evelyn's proposal is that a wide swath of ground be cleared between industry and the city and that a belt of sweet-smelling trees be planted. This idea is perhaps no more idealistic than the greenbelt proposals of modern city planners, but it is considerably more naive, revealing Evelyn's failure to see how deeply entrenched were the commercial and industrial interests in this part of the city and how very much the little inventions and experiments which interested him were doing to encourage these developments on a massive scale.

To place Evelyn properly in the history of technology is something of a problem. It has already been suggested that he comes too early to belong to the Industrial Revolution. The Hammonds place this vast change at the time of the passage of the old village (in the 18th century), the transformation of the textile and pottery industries, and the concentration of capital in the iron, steel, and coal industries.[12] In 1702 Thomas Savery described a steam engine or "Miner's Friend" which Wolf calls "the first practicable steam engine," [13] though its boilers were too weak and its operation was costly. Not until the mid-1780's did Watt's engine, on which so much money and so much time were spent, begin to find users enough to turn a profit. One significant date for the iron industry, however, falls closer to Evelyn's life—1709, when Abraham Darby (the son) first successfully used coal in a blast furnace. (Before this time charcoal had been used, since there was no way to keep the coal fumes from damaging the molten iron.) But the other significant dates for the iron industry fall much later—1776, when the steam engine was used to provide the blast for furnaces, and 1783, when Henry Cort applied coal to the forge and invented puddling and rolling. Pottery making in the 17th century was a simple peasant industry with almost primitive equipment, and though by the end of the century salt-glazing began (it caused dense black smoke) the real industrialization here came in the 1700's. Much the same is true in textiles: new looms were developed in the 17th century, but no important improvements in running them mechanically came until the 18th.

In *Technics and Civilization,* Lewis Mumford takes a very broad look at the history of technology, and his phrase, "Paleotechnic age," may serve our purposes better than "Industrial Revolution." "Technics," too, is a particularly useful term for the study of Evelyn: a word more common in Europe than in America, it refers to the critical, philosophical attempt to determine the place of technology in human affairs, the evaluation of both the good and bad effects of the machine, and suggestions and warnings for future development and control. It is to these areas that men like Evelyn, Defoe, Franklin, and Thoreau gave so much attention, with such mixed success. Mumford borrowed the idea of dividing the history of technology into stages from the 19th century Scots biologist-economist, Patrick Geddes, whose own division comprised the archeological stage (which Mumford calls the "Eotechnic"), the primitive ("Paleotechnic") stage, and the modern ("Neotechnic") stage. In England, the Eotechnic period reached its final stages midway through the 17th century with the beginning of modern experimental science and the achievement of a high degree of efficiency in the use of water and wind power. This period, which has its roots in the dimmest past, is described by Mumford as a "water and wood" complex, and wood is both a universal material and, as for Evelyn, a symbol of the life of man.[14] This period is further marked by the achievement of a fine balance between the crafts and agriculture, with neither functioning at the expense of the other.

Mumford uses "Neotechnic" to describe the modern age, when electricity becomes the primary source of energy, science is being put to ever wider applications, and such civilizing influences as gardens, parks, painting, music, and the theatre reassert themselves impressively. Although there have been periods of rapid technological growth at many different stages of history in different parts of the world, "Paleotechnic," with respect to Western civilization, embraces roughly the late 17th, 18th, and 19th centuries. This period is marked by a growing stress on the accumulation of things, by a determination to mechanize Nature for man's benefit, by the experimental method, and by a decline in the relative importance of art and religion. Capitalism develops at this time, a reflection of expanding markets and the demands of heavy industries like mining and iron making. Both of these industries are, of course, a threat to the natural order, and the struggle of the ironmaker and the forester over wood for fuel is a dominant note in *Sylva*. (The needs of commercial interests for ships pose yet another threat to forests.) A further mark of the Paleotechnic age, especially in its later stages, is the use of steam power. The smoke about which Evelyn complains is not the smoke of the 19th century Coketown, but the age in which he lived had obviously committed itself to a course that could spawn only increasingly rapid and influential technological advances. Evelyn was interested in all these developments; at the same time he recognized that a very precious part of life was being threatened.

It is not hard to see in how many ways Evelyn's books and pamphlets grow out of the tensions created by this vast historical change and reveal the efforts of a dawn man to adjust to technological developments which he cannot really understand, which excite him, and which he somehow sees as a very mixed blessing. Here, on the one hand, is a man interested in gardens, forests, wood carving, and antique coins; on the other, a man making contributions to the redesigning of London, fascinated by experiments at the Royal Society, involved in commerce as its self-appointed historian and in war as a kind of early veterans' administrator. In *Sylva* the eotechnic farmer fights the paleotechnic craftsman who threatens his woods and fields, and in Evelyn's work for Greenwich Hospital a gentle, wood-born man struggles within a bureaucracy to preserve human values lost or threatened by the wars arising from commercial and political expansion. It is time now to examine in more detail the interests of Evelyn which suggest the extent of his commitment to the great revolution that was being born.

III

Some of Evelyn's keenest insights into the needs of his age are embodied in a list of desiderata which he sent to his life-long friend and patron, Sidney Godolphin, in 1696 (Letters, III, 354–8). The idea of a formal treatise on medals will not strike the modern reader as very significant (though Evelyn argues that medals are a valuable historical record), but other suggestions have considerable merit. His proposal for a trade council to protect commerce, encourage manufacturing, and study new inventions; his suggestion that less building be done in London in order to reduce the drain on English capital; his urgent appeal for the discovery of new sources of mechanical power; his pleas for the reform of courts, parliamentary elections, and the penal code—all of these indicate a considerable awareness on his part of the pressures of his age. A list of the posts he held at one time or another again suggests his close ties with embryonic industrialization: both before and after the Great Fire he served on committees for redesigning and rebuilding London; he was a member of commissions for saltpeter (required in ammunition), regulation of the Mint, and foreign plantations; for a time he was a privy-seal commissioner; and he had a long and honorable period of service on behalf of war veterans. His letters suggest (perhaps through design) that both in the 1640's and after the Restoration he was deeply immersed in politics; at the same time they reveal a man who had remained essentially uninvolved and uncommitted. For while many of his contemporaries were dedicating their lives and their fortunes to either the royal or the parliamentary cause, Evelyn wrote to a friend, "I wish you could advise me how I may prevent an absolute ruin as to some part of my fortune, which I would most willingly dispose of in some more peaceable and sober corner of the earth" (Letters, III, 35).

These interests make Evelyn a fair example of the "projector," a typical paleotechnic phenomenon, with ties in one direction to the 17th century virtuoso and in another with the 19th century inventor. Without the philosophical bent of the virtuoso or the inventor's flair for tinkering, the projector developed a towering optimism about the wide applicability of natural knowledge to all kinds of human problems. Franklin, the very archetype of all projectors, surpassed Evelyn in both knowledge of Nature and a sense of the practicality of his schemes. He was, moreover, considerably more persuasive in presenting his plans, and he did not suffer so acutely from that weakness of vision which Evelyn appears to have passed on to Lemuel Gulliver. The projector's point of view is to be seen clearly in Evelyn when he observes, in the essay on solitude and public employment, "The commendation of a true Christian consists in doing, not

in meditating only." [15] Many men in the Renaissance debated the question of the active and the contemplative life,
the wiser usually favoring the life of the mind or some combination of the two worlds. Few so patently used the theme
as a means of announcing their personal availability. Evelyn's choice suggests his intellectual limitations, though it
must be admitted that what he did was far from insignificant. As a projector, he interested himself especially in
(1) the problems of commerce and the crafts, including the
commercial wars and the attendant problems of veterans and
workers; (2) the growth of the Royal Society; (3) problems
involving libraries and museums; and (4) the development
of the 17th century city.

There are many references in the Diary to Evelyn's interest in shipping problems and in trade, and eventually a book
was produced, *Navigation and Commerce, their Original and
Progress* (1674). As the title suggests, this is one of the many
interminable histories which Evelyn conceived. Very little
insight into 17th century commercial problems is offered,
however, and the general level of the book is indicated by
Evelyn's suggestion that the earth was disposed from the
beginning to commerce "because it offers so many objects of
utility and delight." Though Evelyn in this book praises the
Dutch for their commercial prowess, the Dutch ambassador
was offended by it and demanded its recall, a request which
Charles II made some attempt to grant (IV, 41). Comment
on the book can rest with the observation that Evelyn saw
commerce much as Ruskin did, as a means by which society
is established, order is maintained, and the blessings of God
are distributed.

Evelyn's interest in crafts and trades is traced by Hiscock

back to his boyhood on the farm, where he was able to observe a wide variety of occupations and skills. This knowledge was doubtless useful in the project he later undertook of compiling a general dictionary of human occupations. He found research something of a problem, however, because of the difficulty of talking to "mechanical capricious" persons. At the time a philosophic club was being considered, Evelyn suggested that the topic of mechanical trades would be worth discussing and thereby laid bare a deep-seated confusion in his own mind about the practical aspects of scientific knowledge. As a traveler, too, he was constantly on the lookout for artisans and craftsmen whom he might observe. Like Howell he was interested in glassmaking, and while he was in Venice he visited the Isle of Murano, which was the center of the European glass blowing industry, though he noted, at the same time, the superiority of glass made at Greenwich (IV, 13; 98). At Tours he saw silk making and was particularly impressed by the machinery (II, 145). At Byflyte he watched the manufacture of paper (IV, 141), a commodity which, as Mumford suggests, is symbolic of the concern of the 17th century with bureaucracy, which feeds on paper work. His interest in construction was great—whether it was the building of the triumphal arches around London for the coronation of Charles II, or the great trade of shipbuilding.

The Diary indicates that Evelyn was well enough acquainted with the famous shipbuilder Pett to dine with him at Chatham and to be shown by this "most skillfull *Naupaegus* in the World" (III, 359) the models which he had built for study. On another occasion he was impressed by "The Charles" and its 120 brass cannon, built by Old Shish, "a plaine honest Carpenter . . . yet one that can give very little account of his art by discourse" (III, 506). There is in Evelyn's description of Shish, who was apparently illiterate, more than a little condescension, none of which is manifest in Evelyn's comments on the new-style, technologically sound builder Withers, whom Evelyn introduced to the King. The great impression which mechanical drawings and technical data made on Evelyn is to be seen in his account of a glorious day when Pepys pulled down from his shelves in the Navy office a folio volume in which complete designs of ships—to the smallest detail—were set forth. Evelyn's comment is characteristic: "I esteeme this one booke above any of the *Sybillas,* & it is an extraordinary Jewel" (IV, 271). Evelyn's concern that shipbuilding be reduced to an exact science is suggestive of the increasing rationalism of his age.[16] And in a more general way the entire expansion of naval and maritime operations is itself symbolic—symbolic of the growing interest of the English in war and commerce, forces which were producing just the type of personality that Evelyn became.

From the beginning of time, war has been a chief nurse of the arts and sciences, and Evelyn reveals considerable interest in this supreme occupation of civilized man. Ponsonby is doubtless quite right when he declares that Evelyn was unheroic by temper and indifferent to the actual art of combat. Nevertheless, when he was in his twenties he served for a brief period in August, 1641, as a listless dilettante in the English forces in the Low Countries, and his account of this experience reveals a considerable interest in weaponry (II, 37, 38). In Paris in 1651 Evelyn visited the Palais Royal, where he was interested in "a Compleate fort, made with Bastions, Graft, halfe moones, ravelins & furnished with greate Gunns" (III, 44). In 1674 Evelyn visited Windsor

Castle, where he witnessed a mock attack upon a fort as well as other maneuvers which would have delighted Uncle Toby, all done, he says, "to the greate satisfaction of a thousand spectators . . . realy very divertisant" (IV, 42). A much more serious interest than these tourist attractions or the personal collection of sieges and battles which Evelyn maintained (III, 37) came with his work on behalf of distressed and wounded soldiers, the ultimate scraps and leavings of the feast of war which the technology of his age served up. As early as 1641 Evelyn records a visit to a hospital for "lame and decrepid souldiers" in Amsterdam (II, 45), but his work began in earnest in 1664, when he was appointed a Commissioner for sick and wounded prisoners anticipated during the coming Dutch War. Evelyn's special charge was to be the ports in Kent and Sussex, but at no time were the funds granted him sufficient for the work he had to do. This meant not only personal financial embarrassment (he petitioned for reimbursement for nearly forty years) but also keen grief that he could do so little to relieve such great need. In 1666 he impressed the Duke of Albemarle with his design for a naval infirmary and later in the year he showed his plans to the king; a site was selected, but then the project was shelved for thirty years. In 1682 he made a trip to Lambeth with Wren and other officials to secure the archbishop's approval of plans for a hospital for "emerited" soldiers, and in 1694 the decision was made to locate the proposed institution at Greenwich. Queen Mary provided the palace and an annual income, Wren supplied free designs, and Evelyn, in 1696, was appointed treasurer at a salary of three hundred pounds.

A second manifestation of Evelyn's concern with the ad-

vancing technology of his age was his interest in the Royal
Society. Though scientifically one of the least distinguished
of the group, Evelyn's fame as a virtuoso, which his literary
activity had promoted, was more than enough to secure his
membership. Evelyn's position in the structure of this society
was an important one: he made early proposals to Robert
Boyle for a *"Mathematical* College" (III, 232); he records
—if somewhat inaccurately—the early meetings; he was
forced to turn down many committee assignments because
of the press of other duties; he was apparently responsible
for the name "Royal Society" (III, 306); and he gave his
concern very sturdy form by a gift of fifty thousand bricks
for the society's building in 1668. On the surface at least his
academic credentials were more than adequate for membership—military science and geography in Holland, medicine
at Padua, chemistry at Paris. But one has only to read the
charges of dilettantism brought against him when he was at
Balliol or his own account of the delightful time he spent
in Paris to suspect that his studies were polite and genteel,
never intellectually exhausting. What is more, Evelyn's descriptions of the experiments which he witnessed at the society's meetings do not suggest any comprehension of the
secrets of Nature, in the Baconian sense, of its power, or of
its minute, detailed operations, which are the province of the
genuine scientist. Evelyn records experiments in the use of
the burning glass, the anatomy of the "camelion," the weight
of atmosphere, the nature of phosphorus, the wind pump,
production of light, the effects of snake bite, growing plants
without earth, the water content of human beings, echoes,
tapeworms, the nourishment of the human embryo, magnets,
surface adhesion of glass, and Roman burial urns. Never,

though, does Evelyn provide the slightest hint that he under-stood what was going on. He was, I believe, a thoroughgoing phenomenalist, concerned almost exclusively with what he could see, possessing no ability and little desire to probe beneath the surface.

The career of that remarkable 17th century economist, Sir William Petty, a man whom Evelyn admired deeply, offers many illuminating similarities and contrasts to Eve-lyn's. After an afternoon visit in 1665 with Petty, Hooke, and Dr. Wilkins, all busy contriving racing wheels, ship rig-gings, and chariots, Evelyn concluded that in Petty he had found one of the most ingenious men in Europe (III, 416). Somewhat later (IV, 56–59; Letters, III, 393) Evelyn pro-vides an account of this genius, who touched so many fields with such great mastery. Finding himself abandoned as a youth in France, Petty learned the language expertly, taught navigation on the Continent, studied medicine at Leyden, and won the friendship of Hobbes in Paris. Back in England he divided his time between the textile mills owned by his father and the study of medicine at Oxford, where he later taught anatomy. Called to reorganize the medical services for the army of Ireland, he eventually became involved in redis-tribution of land in Ireland and thereby the author of the first modern land survey, a massive piece of scholarship which was eventually published at a cost of £1,000. In 1659 Petty was involved in the ruin of Cromwell's government, but he came to prominence again during the Restoration and devoted himself to problems of government finance, sta-tistics, and the census. He was a member of the Rota, a friend of Pepys, and a frequent contributor to discussions at the Royal Society. One of his inventions, a double-bottomed

boat, particularly interested Evelyn (IV, 58; III, 392). I
know of no source of information about Petty's inner life. It
may be that he sacrificed it even more fully than Evelyn did
in order to master, as he did, the outer world.

An interesting facet of the kind of mind to be seen so mag-
nificently in Petty and to a lesser degree in Evelyn is a peculiar susceptibility to making collections—sometimes of
significant natural objects, sometimes of mere curiosities.
The 17th century was one of the great acquisitive ages, and
in part at least the drive to collect can be ascribed to a desire
to preserve the past. This fact suggests, in turn, that a sense
of the past was being lost, and—if we may follow Mumford
—a fear that life was becoming too complex, too far out of
touch with its roots. Men who cannot live as vitally as they
would care to may, in museums, at least look at the evidence
of more heroic ages. Or they may, as Ernest Schachtel suggests, use the museum to protect themselves from direct encounter with the living or the heroic. During his European
tour Evelyn visited many notable collections of curiosities:
at Leyden, for instance, he saw exotic plants, animal skeletons, mummies, Chinese curios, and a knife taken from a
drunken Dutchman's "guts." At the home of one Roman
virtuoso he saw precious stones, medals, and a folding lad-
der; elsewhere in the city he saw Roman keys and rings, a
nail from Nero's house, bronze hinges from Corinth, and a
seaman's skin. In Florence he saw collections of antique
heads, a piece of gold as big as an egg, crocodiles, elks, and
other preserved animals. In Venice there was a notable collection of petrified eggs, hedgehogs, and sponges, and Paris
offered, among its treasures, a dromedary, a ropedancer, and
a water spouter.

English taste in curios seems to have been somewhat less exotic. In one enthusiastic passage from the Diary (III, 106), Evelyn describes the rare things to be seen at Oxford —thousands of manuscripts in nineteen languages from Laud's library, the Koran on a sheet of calico, Joseph's many-colored coat, a collection of Russian whips, mathematical instruments and skeletons, Dr. Wilkins' transparent apiaries, a gallery of shadows, dials, and perspectives, a "way-wise," thermometers, balances, cunning locks, and watches. During his English travels he came upon a sheep with six legs (five of which it used in walking), a goose with four legs, a hairy maid who later married and produced a child that was not hairy, Siamese twins (of whom Evelyn drew a picture), ship models, a curious clock with the signs of the Zodiac, an engine for weaving silk stockings, rarities brought from Japan by the Jesuits, that "melancholy water fowl" the pelican, and, in London, an hermaphrodite. Among the notable 17th century collections which Evelyn visited were those of Dr. Hans Sloane (especially concerned with the natural history of Jamaica), which formed the nucleus of the British Museum; the "innumerable curiosities" of that "ingenious person" Mr. Hartlib; the Queen's collection of medals, statues, china screens, and gold plates; and that at Hampton Court, which included curious insects, tiny puppies, ship models, and the design for a perpetual-motion machine. In his work on the preservation of the Arundel Marbles, Evelyn himself made a remarkable contribution of the past, a contribution for which he was properly honored by Oxford.[17] It is easy to smile at the strange things in which Evelyn expressed interest, but behind his often abortive enthusiasms there lies the genuine perplexity of an intelligent man about what was really significant, what was trivial. The problem of the direction of knowledge faced every thinking man of the 17th Century.

To the problems of still another acquisitive institution, the library, Evelyn devoted much time and made a considerable contribution. Although the history of libraries appears to be older than that of museums, the coming of modern times, with the enormous increase in the number of books and the complexity of the language, brought new problems to the collectors of great numbers of books. Evelyn's own bibliographic enthusiasm emerges when he describes a visit to the royal library at Whitehall, where he was bored by the exotic curiosities but so enthralled by the illuminated manuscripts and the books on medals that he spent half a week there, "locked up, & alone amongst these bookes" (IV, 216). Evelyn also records visits to the Vatican Library in Rome; to the incomparable library of Lord Spenser, which was judged to have the best collection in Europe of mathematical books; and to Bishop Stillingfleet's library, which he declared the finest in London (Letters, III, 307). Evelyn's interest in encouraging reading led him to propose that a supply of books published in the city be maintained in the West Portico of St. Paul's, with membership in this early book club to be open to every apprentice in London. Proposals like this have been a favorite with projectors: Franklin suggested a similar scheme for Philadelphia. Evelyn's idea apparently attracted some attention, for he notes in his Diary (IV, 367) that he has asked Tenison to assist Wren in erecting a public library to lure young boys into books and away from taverns and coffee houses.

Still another evidence of Evelyn's interest in making books

more readily available was his translation of one of the very early books on library science, Gabriel Naudé's *Avis pour Dresser une Bibliothèque*. The original appeared in 1627; Evelyn's translation, *On Establishing a Library*, in 1661.[18] Even the curiously superficial reason given by Naudé for creating libraries—"because he has a library, he may with reason call himself a cosmopolite or citizen of the whole world"—is the kind that would appeal to Evelyn. The contents of the book are not notable in themselves, nor are they especially indicative of Evelyn's interests except as they suggest his concern with the growing problem of keeping track of an increasingly complex mass of materials. In this respect the contents clearly bespeak early modern times. Among the topics discussed are book selection, the importance of every kind of book—even commonplace books—to the buyer, methods of book procurement, the building, location and arrangement of libraries. One positive result of Evelyn's interest in bibliographic problems was that he assumed responsibility for the books presented by the Duke of Norfolk to the Royal Society.[19]

Evelyn's interest in books had still another facet—a life-long concern with the quality of books being issued by the English presses. His point of view is clearly spelled out in a letter to Lord Chancellor Clarendon (Letters, III, 189), in which he complains that English stationers and printers were attempting to make as large a profit as possible, and that their products were notably inferior to continental books. While Evelyn does commend Bentley for the press which he was establishing at Cambridge, his highest praise is reserved for the great presses on the Continent—the Elzevirian Press in Leyden and the Plantine Shop in Antwerp. Of special concern to Evelyn was the generally poor quality of illustrations in English books. (An exception was the work done by the English bookseller William London, whose books on natural history were notable for their clear and accurate prints.) The significance of Evelyn's concern becomes quite clear in the dedication of his book *Sculptura* (1662) to the Royal Society. This book, which Evelyn calls a history of chalcography (the art of engraving on brass), was publicized as a discussion of the way by which scientists could, through illustrations, present their ideas more clearly. Basically it presents a technique for mezzotint engraving which Evelyn claimed to have introduced into England to solve the problem of proper shading. One of the worst books that Evelyn wrote, *Sculptura,* is marred by long pages of etymologizing, meaningless lists of painters, and endless laments about the dice, dogs, and mistresses on which men who ought to have been patronizing the arts were spending their money. Throughout this book Evelyn is lavish in his praise of pictures as an educational device, declaring illustrations "superior to all those *Abstracted termes,* and *secondary intentions* wherewith *Masters* commonly torment and weary their tender and weak Capacities." [20] The complexity of this book is so great as to suggest that Evelyn himself was far from master of the material, but the theme significantly underscores Evelyn's distinctly sensory orientation and points up a fundamental problem of the modern world—the problem of the dissemination of highly factual knowledge about complex structures and processes.

A fourth area in which Evelyn's concern with technological problems is manifest is the development of the early-modern city. Evelyn's interest in the nature of the city goes

back at least as far as 1641, when he visited the Low Countries, and 1643–1647, when he made his extended continental
tour. During these years Evelyn became well acquainted
with Amsterdam, Paris, Rome, and Naples, among other
places. What he had to say by way of personal observation is
difficult to separate from the comments of other travelers
whose work he copied and from his own constant comments
on the various art and curio collections which he visited. His
observations, moreover, are usually diffuse and ill-arranged,
lacking the depth of analysis and the sense of important issues which characterizes the work of modern students of the
city. What he normally notes are the width and condition of
the streets, the tree plantings, and the size and condition of
the public buildings, hospitals, churches, and gardens. Renaissance Amsterdam is of the greatest interest to students of
urban development because of the way it was fanning out on
all sides from a central core (the dock area). Evelyn is not
aware of this pattern of growth, though he was obviously
impressed by the prodigious amount of shipping which the
port handled. He comments from Naples on the fine paving
of the streets and the general air of magnificence; he is impressed by the all-pervasive secular spirit in Haarlem; and
he describes the famous arsenal in Venice (which had impressed Dante too) as "one of the best furnish'd in the
World" (II, 456). The odd garb of many of the Venetians
and the pomp with which their lives were surrounded—both
well-known facts—also receive attention. Ferrara he found
ugly but impressive for its public works, a comment that confirms Burckhardt's observation that it was at this time the
most modern and efficiently administered city in Italy. Rome
appears to have dazzled Evelyn—"resolv'd I was to spend no

moment idly here" (II, 213), but from his long account no
clear picture except that of the harried tourist emerges. But
even though the accounts of foreign cities in the Diary leave
much to be desired, Evelyn was accumulating a fund of
knowledge and insight which were to be of immense value
when he grew interested in the specific problems of redesigning London.

Comments on London fog and smoke are rarely missing
for long from the pages of the Diary. Evelyn speaks frequently of being engulfed in "the thickest fog in the memory
of man" and of the fact that such fog was impenetrable even
with torches. His bitterness over this offense to eye and ear
eventually led to the publication of his pamphlet *Fumifugium,* which, as I have suggested already, seems to be particularly symbolic of the peculiar role and point of view that
this chapter is finding in Evelyn. Evelyn begins this essay
with a brief—and I should think telling—argument ad-
dressed to the king, in which he contrasts the smoke pouring
over the royal palace in London with the sweet smells issuing
from the palace gardens of the great continental capitals.
Warming to his theme, Evelyn notes how distressingly few
have been the civic improvements in London over the centuries: bricks and wood continue to be the dominant building
materials, misshapen houses and ugly warehouses everywhere meet the eye, and the streets are poorly paved and
twisted. London, Evelyn complains, was not even profiting
by the advice to be found in the Roman architect Vitruvius
(which Burton had reviewed) concerning the pernicious
influence of bad air, and this is the greater tragedy, says
Evelyn, because of the city's fine natural site. But everywhere he finds the atmosphere polluted by a "hellish and dis-

mall cloud of sea-coal" which tarnished metals, caused pulmonary disease, obscured and dirtied public buildings, and ruined trees and flowers. Clothes hung on hedgerows were quickly dirtied, and there was a carelessness about control of the nuisance which reminded Evelyn forcibly of the rigid policing undertaken in Florence by the dyers. Evelyn's naive suggestion that a belt of trees be planted around the city to cut down the smoke has already been noted; much more to the point is his proposal for zoning laws—specifically that breweries, lime-burning plants, and other works that produced heavy smoke be forced outside the city. It seems to be generally recognized today that adequate zoning is an absolute necessity for adequately functioning cities.

Evelyn's interest in the restoration of London goes back at least to 1659, when, in his *Character of England,* he criticized the narrow streets and the asymmetrical arrangement of the city, as well as the large number of poorly designed buildings.[21] In 1662 Evelyn was appointed to a committee charged with repaving the London streets, and his proposals for a city of "Beauty, commodiousness, and magnificence" were submitted just a few days before the fire. His plans were forgotten in the rush to rebuild the city, but the span and scope of his involvement reflects his deep concern with this facet of the advancing technology of his age.

The plans submitted by Wren and Evelyn just after the Fire were similar in many features, despite the fact that it is thought they were drawn up separately.[22] Both called for radical changes in the street plans so as to create many interlocking spoke systems. The fact that Evelyn's plans were not adopted does not obviate their value, since his proposals would have been very expensive and would have delayed the

rebuilding of the city. In particular, the fact that old foundations survived, strong enough to support new buildings, made
changes in the street plans impossible. Bell suggests that the
plans laid out by Evelyn would have produced a London with
a decidedly continental flavor—a stately waterfront, a cen-
trally located Guildhall, and clusters of public buildings.
Under Evelyn's proposal, many neighborhoods would have
been established, each with its own wide piazza (square,
oval, or round) to create "views," each piazza including its
own fountain of crystal waters and encircled by buildings
arranged so as to create a beautiful skyline. Evelyn's personal vigor seems to lie behind the suggestion that the architecture of the trade halls ought to be "of the most refined
Gusto," and his love of display appears in his recommenda-
tion that the main streets should be one hundred feet wide
—a width regarded by modern authorities as self-defeating
and wasteful. Like Wren, Evelyn suggests the banishment of
naval works, breweries, and other industries to special sections of the city. Bell calls Evelyn's design a stone city of
"daring impracticality," but it is evident, I think, that Evelyn's was no "poetical commonwealth" such as Burton
dreamed of. His contention that his plans would make London "fitter for commerce, apter for government, sweeter for
health, more glorious for beauty" reveals an understanding
of the city's function that a modern urban theoretician might
well be proud of.

   This insight into a city's human and practical purposes
carries over into a communal feeling which emerges—among
other places—in his account of the Great Fire: he is deeply
moved, for instance, by the throngs "ready to perish for
hunger & destitution, yet not asking one penny for reliefe"

(III, 461), and no reader can be untouched by the comment that he "went againe to the ruines, for it was now no longer a Citty" (III, 462). Evelyn seems to have sensed intuitively, too, the profound communal wisdom behind the system of tiny almshouses (each holding half a dozen or so sick and poor) which many benefactors had established throughout the city and which he frequently visited on missions of charity.[23] They were no doubt inefficient, but in the way they must have fostered a genuinely meaningful life for the wretched, they stood in sharp contrast to the vast designs of institutionalized charity which occupied so much of Evelyn's attention.

IV

Evelyn's desire for a London that would be clean and spacious, beautifully adapted to the gently sloping terrain on which it sat, suited in every way for commerce and government, stood in bold opposition to the prevailing needs of the advancing "paleotechnic" age in which he was also very deeply involved.[24] Pragmatic considerations decreed that when the city was rebuilt, the narrow, twisted streets be preserved and all the rich human contacts created by piazzas and the neighborhood plan of city design be eliminated. Clearly the spirit of Bacon, who had appeared to de-emphasize art and religion and to put a heavy stress on technological progress, was triumphing. Nevertheless, Evelyn continued to speak out in behalf of loveliness and refinement, though he was frequently offended by the increasing ugliness he saw all about him. His observations, made over a period of many years, need to be collected now and put in some kind of order.

Evelyn's Diary and the accounts of other English travelers in France and Italy at this time indicate clearly that the late Renaissance city, however much it was devoting itself to commerce, had by no means turned its back completely on beauty, either natural or man-made. One particularly striking manifestation of the continental aesthetic sense could be seen in the many occasions which dotted the calendar for pomp and ceremony, and public display. The eternally primitive in Evelyn never lets a procession go by unnoticed. In Paris, from the window of "Mr. *Hobbs,* the famous *Philosopher* of Malmsbury" (III, 41), he sees a cavalcade pass through the streets, and he describes the antique costumes at a court masque as "stupendiously rich & glorious" (III, 32). In Venice Evelyn witnessed the jollity of Ascension Week Fair, as noblemen and their wives tramped through the streets on stilts, and he long remembered too the "quiet & solemn" Shrove Tuesday pageant there (III, 1). In Rome on Palm Sunday, 1645, he witnessed a procession and Papal mass, and on Christmas Eve of 1644 he went from church to church all night long to see the pageantry and the nativity scenes set out by the friars (II, 385, 290). At home in England he participated in a procession at Oxford, "all of us rob'd in Scarlet, with Caps & hoods &c." (III, 535). And on various occasions in London he saw the magnificent Thames procession when the new queen was brought to London for the first time in 1662 and an equestrian display for the visiting Russian ambassador, whose behavior, apparently, was as bad as that of his 20th century successors. The climax to a lifetime of display hunting came, however, at the coronation of Charles II, which Evelyn, partly from newspaper accounts, describes in detail (III, 278 ff.). Through his eyes the procession becomes almost visible to ours—the royal train "as rich as *Embroidery, velvet, Cloth* of *Gold* & *Sil:* & Jewells could make them & their pransing horses," the "blew cloth" from the west door of the abbey to Westminster Stairs, the triumphant barge, and the "extraordinary feasting" at Whitehall. Such grand, cheerful, and moving sights continued throughout the 17th Century in England to be a source of beauty, despite the increasing ugliness of the city. And Evelyn's wholehearted response suggests at once something quite juvenile and some profound ability to identify himself with the community through its public rituals.

Evelyn appears to have responded to the fine arts with much less freedom, much less emotion. He was a rank amateur about painting, an amateur whose tastes and skill had advanced very little beyond the stage of childhood dabbling. In his grand tour of the Continent he visited most of the greatest treasure houses and galleries—St. Denis, the Louvre, and the Luxembourg Palace in Paris; the Vatican, Farnese Galleries, and the Sistine Chapel in Rome; the Uffizi Galleries in Florence; and San Marco in Venice. In Rotterdam Evelyn became acquainted with a peculiar style of art appreciation practiced by the Dutch—financial speculation in fine painting. This was a combination of art and economics that he found very neat indeed. Back home in England Evelyn visited many of the great private collections, seeing at Hampton Court the rare pictures and incomparable furniture, and at Windsor and Montagu frescoes which exceeded anything, he says, done by Virio. His preference for the furniture in the Duchess of Portsmouth's dressing room to the sight of the duchess dressing has called down upon him the scorn of Mr. Hiscock, who seems to be convinced that such indifference to feminine beauty makes Evelyn less a man—or at least a less honest man—than Pepys.

Two important facets of Evelyn's interest in art—his pronounced fondness for landscapes and his tendency to evaluate paintings in terms of their "photographic" realism—will hardly raise his status among sophisticated modern readers. The taste for landscapes has been traced by Mr. DeBeer to Evelyn's country boyhood; I think it was rooted also in Evelyn's generally optimistic outlook on his world. As for realism, it appears to have been the chief—if not the only—standard of painting among Evelyn's contemporaries, who found, according to Bell, fair "records of appearances useful and pleasing." Such a point of view led Evelyn to praise a statue at Delft for being as big as life and a Raphael because the "earnestnesse of the Secretary looking on in expectation of what he was next to write, is so to life, & so naturall" (IV, 102). That his taste was somewhat baffled by Michelangelo's Last Judgment is evident by his description: "miraculous . . . considering the multitudes of Nakeds, & variety of posture." The ceiling of the Sistine Chapel he dismissed as "full of rare worke" (II, 298).

Evelyn's interest in the minor arts was intense, and because of their scope, which his mind was able to encompass, his judgments are generally reliable.[25] Indeed, he is much better when he talks of painting as a decorative art than as an interpretive or analytical one. While in Europe he sought out Marc Antonio, a famous enamelist, visited an artist known for his skill in perspectives and in ivory, and watched at their work a goldsmith, the landscape painter Perelle, and a copper engraver. At Tostes he watched workers in ivory, tortoise shells, and sea shells, and back in London he chatted with one Mr. Cooper, an engraver, while he was occupied with a crayon drawing of the head of the King. Evelyn speaks enthusiastically of the wood carving in the sacristy at Bologna, and he was himself responsible for the discovery of Grinling Gibbons, England's greatest woodcarver. Evelyn records his discovery of Gibbons in the Diary entry for January 18, 1671 (III, 567), noting that he first saw Gibbons at work in a solitary cottage copying in wood Tintoretto's. Crucifixion. This carving, which Gibbons offered for £100, Evelyn praises very highly: "nothing even in nature so tender, & delicate as the flowers & festoones about it." On the first of March the King saw this piece at Whitehall, and eventually Gibbons got further work from the King at Windsor as well as major commissions from Wren. Behind Evelyn's interest in Gibbons lies much more than pride in a protégé—once again there is an indication of the profound satisfaction which Evelyn took in the manipulation of wood, in the feel and smell of lumber, in memories of the forest.

About the minor arts there has always been this ambiguity: no artist of the first magnitude and of absolute greatness has ever limited himself to them, nor has any critic of the first rank ever made them his chief study. The proportions are too unheroic, the materials (paper, wood, clay, ivory, gold) do not present the physical opposition of virtually unyielding marble, the subtleties of oil, or the sheer intellectual challenge of music. The manipulative skill on which the minor arts so heavily rely would seem to work almost at cross purposes with anything fostering true greatness of spirit. On the other hand, it is pottery, wood carving, weaving, and furniture that surround a sensitive man every day, beautifying and lending grace to his normal routine as the major arts—by their very grandeur and expensiveness—cannot. Such a feeling for the gentle, subtle, nonoverwhelming way in which art can touch the life of a man who wishes—and can afford—to have it around him lies behind a note that Evelyn strikes persistently—the obligation of the man of intelligence, wealth, and leisure to patronize the arts. Evelyn would have made a splendid Oriental. Nothing can more aptly symbolize the ambiguity of his moral and personal stature than the hold which the minor arts, not grandly spiritual, not products of the keenest perceptions, but gracious parts of the daily routine, had upon him.

Curiously, though, Evelyn is at his very best in his comments on architecture, the grandest of all the major arts. Evelyn's success here may lie in the fact that the art of building neatly combines aesthetics and technology, or it may point to his willingness to abandon current standards when they seemed to threaten human values. Although Evelyn had no technical training, his intense interest in architecture is suggested by a charming note in the Diary in which he describes how (like Ruskin in Italy) he scrambled over the fine stone roof of King's College Chapel, studying the details of its construction (III, 138). In an age when, as Traill notes, more and more building was being done by professionals, Evelyn continued to uphold the older Renaissance role of the man of cultivated tastes doubling as critic and designer. His talents put him in some demand as an assessor of fine properties, and the comments on great houses which he recorded are probably freer than those he made to proud owners. The garden of John Berkley's London home he found incomparable, but the kitchen and stables were ill-placed and the corridors had "no report to the wings they joyne to" (III, 625). (Interior vistas through the whole house were as highly regarded as long garden perspectives.) Evelyn found the Lord Chancellor's house "the best contrived, the most useful, graceful and magnificent" in England (Letters, III, 177), and he is high in his praise of the Lord Chamberlain's house, which he found commodious, magnificent, graced with a splendid staircase, and all the more overwhelming because it had been created (at great expense) from older houses. Among other things which Evelyn notes were the extraordinary neatness of the Earl of Sunderland's house at Althorp; the yew-parqueted floor and the oval central hall with cupola at the Earl of Essex's house, Cassiobury Place; the Palladian balustrades and wainscoting of Spanish oak in the King's house at Euston; and the richly gilded and frescoed double-cube dining room in Wilton House, which belonged to the Earl of Pembroke. Evelyn's frequent comment that a house was in itself magnificent, but that it sat upon a wretched site, suggests a truly human, Vitruvian conception of the total problem of the architect, which was to provide in the fullest possible way for all of the physical and aesthetic needs of a noble style of life.

Evelyn's work for the committee charged with consideration of the problems of St. Paul's Cathedral seems to have been of near-professional calibre. The cathedral's condition at mid-century was woeful: the tower was leaning outward (though there was some suspicion that it had been built out of plumb), its pillars were settling, and its stone was moldering.[26] In an interesting passage in the Diary (III, 449), Evelyn describes the way the committee plumbed the uprights and debated what course to take: both Evelyn and Wren supported entirely new construction (at least of the steeple), whereas Mr. Prat and Mr. Chichley argued for repairs only. But apparently both Evelyn and Wren had in mind an entirely new plan, too, a church with a cupola, "a forme of church building, not as yet knowne in England, but of wonderfull grace" (III, 449). As DeBeer points out, almost none of Evelyn's or Wren's suggestions were adopted, and the Fire, of course, made all the arguments for remodeling completely academic. With good grace Evelyn describes the first Sunday in the new St. Paul's (December 5, 1697), the choir at this time being completely finished and the new organ one of the best in Europe (V, 278).

Evelyn's useful translation (1664) of Fréard de Chambray's *Parallèle de l'Architecture Antique et de la Moderne* (1650) (to which he added some years later his own *Account of Architects and Architecture*) grew out of his complaint that unlearned masons who bore responsibility for the design of great buildings needed a grammar or a primer for their trade. Although Evelyn was in this volume translating an author who had himself relied heavily on Vitruvius, the book seems to offer a valid insight into Evelyn's ideas, few of which were original anyway. Evelyn, for instance, accepts de Chambray's view that architecture is essentially a study of proportion and therefore that clean, simple buildings are best. From his early days Evelyn had disliked Gothic architecture, describing it as heavy, dark, melancholy, lacking due proportion, use, or beauty.[27] But as Lovejoy and DeBeer have noted, there is considerable ambiguity about Evelyn's use of the term "Gothic." (He was not, as has been thought, the first to use it in English, but the Diary has been a convenient place to find it.) Lovejoy observes that Evelyn applies the term to buildings erected both by the Goths and the Arabs, buildings that were on the one hand dark and heavy, on the other hand erected on slender pillars and decorated with lacy cutwork.[28] DeBeer notes that Evelyn applies "Gothic" to early Christian, Byzantine, and Romanesque architecture, as well as to the medieval pointed style.[29] Further confusion is engendered by Evelyn's description of S. Maria Maggiore as of mixed design—modern (by which he meant, says DeBeer, revived classicism) and antique (or the style of classical antiquity). And from a man who obviously enjoyed Baroque (he called the façade of S. Maria Vittoria "ravishing" and thought St. Peter's stupendous and incomparable), the condemnation of "busy and Gothic triflings" sounds strange indeed. Evelyn's preference for lines of classical simplicity obviously yielded to the impact of High Renaissance Baroque, just as his dislike of the medieval cathedral was sometimes offset by his affection for the romantic gloom in which Gothic piles were invariably steeped. These inconsistencies are the result of lack of technical knowledge or—for once—of an overstrong emotional response. Neither is an unforgivable sin, and both are offset by broad appreciation which Evelyn so often conveys for the values of fine buildings. When he suggests that architecture —because of the great sum of knowledge it demands— should be a university discipline, not merely a trade for mechanics, he was speaking prophetically and paying himself a richly deserved compliment. One need only scan the pages of Vitruvius's *Ten Books of Architecture* to see how right Evelyn was, to see how vast, how deeply rooted in the human situation the problems of "right building" are.

v

To embark at this point on a full discussion of Evelyn's many and complex social relationships would be a grave error in proportion. In a general way Ponsonby has covered adequately the whole field; Clara Marburg has assembled the facts about Evelyn's relations with Pepys; and Mr. Hiscock, in two carefully documented books based on unpublished materials, has presented a picture of Evelyn's dealings with members of his family and with Mrs. Godolphin. A good many of Evelyn's friendships were based on his own deep-seated emotional needs; almost all were marred in one way or another by grave blunders. These needs and these blunders reveal a great deal about Evelyn's character. Thus we may say, for instance, that if Evelyn was damned upon his death, it was for an astonishing array of the most minor of minor sins. Jealous pique is to be seen in his comment when he was passed over for membership in the Privy Seal Commission: "I think I might have ben one of them, had I thought it seasonable" (V, 7). An incredible superficiality and materialism lay behind his shocking comment on one Mr. Creech, a clergyman (and translator of Lucretius) who committed suicide; Evelyn is puzzled, "for besides one of the best fellowships in the University, he had a living, I am told worth 200 pounds per ann." (V, 417).[30] Personal hurt is reflected in a comment about some unrequited kindnesses to Bishop Cosin, "which he little remembred in his greatnesse" (III, 355). And a sharp tongue is pointed at the Quakers ("a Melancholy proud sort of people, & exceedingly ignorant"— III, 179) and at the Puritans (men "of high flight, and above Ordinances"—III, 204).

His devotion to Margaret Blagge, a saint among the court ladies, extended from 1672, through her courtship by Godolphin, until her death following childbirth in 1678. This relationship, which seems to have centered around such harmless activities as dining together, letter writing, saying prayers, and exchanging advice on personal matters, had beneath its surface the almost vicious determination of an already married man to dominate a young girl and to cut her off from the joys of normal love, all in the name of religion. Despite his grief at her death, Evelyn appears to have been relieved when the tremendous demands made by their relationship could cease. He soothed his feelings by writing a series of yearly commemorative volumes about her, as a means of extracting patronage money from her husband, Sidney. In no other relationship is the possessiveness he felt for Margaret revealed. His friendships with Boyle, Pepys, and other members of the Royal Society seem to have been entirely honest and forthright. Pepys has been described as the one close friend Evelyn had; clearly he trusted Evelyn deeply, for he imparted to him some exceedingly rare morsels of gossip, including information about the secret religious convictions of Charles II (IV, 476).

There are some puzzling facets to Evelyn's relationship with Jeremy Taylor, whom he heard preach for the first time on May 7, 1654 (III, 95), and whom he very quickly made his counselor in spiritual matters. What Taylor could have said to Evelyn by way of advice is hard to imagine, and their tenuous relationship must have been marked by embarrassing silence on many points. When Taylor visited Sayes Court, he congratulated Evelyn on the delightful appointments, but even more on being above them (Letters, III, 71). Every bit of evidence indicates, however, that Evelyn, far from being above his worldly comforts, was really deeply immersed in them, and that Taylor was probably keen enough to see this. Nevertheless, the reply comes back from

Evelyn that he takes little satisfaction in the delights of his estate and would abandon them "if I found that they did in the least distract my thoughts from better things." In all fairness it must be noted that the letters which Taylor and Evelyn exchanged at a time when they had both lost children are among the most touching and sincere in our language. When the complete picture of Evelyn's relationships with people is seen, however, it would appear that the "It" about which Martin Buber talks—rather than the "Thou"—was the dominant factor.

In his essay "Of Studies" Bacon draws a useful distinction between the "particulars" which "expert men can execute, and perhaps judge of . . . one by one" and "the general counsels, and the plots and marshallings of affairs" which are best managed by learned men. More recently Alfred North Whitehead has observed that professional training in specific, limited areas is one of the great facts of the modern world. But with the rapid progress which such training has made possible there has come also, he laments, an unfortunate situation: the fact that "the task of coordination is left to those who lack either the force or the character to succeed in some definite career. In short, the specialized functions of the community are performed better and more progressively, but the generalized direction lacks vision." [31] Evelyn, it would seem, was by temperament and natural gifts born to be one of those suited to "general counsels" and "marshallings of affairs." If he was an expert in anything, it was in horticulture, a field that with every passing year was becoming (proportionally) a less and less important part of the life of men. But even as a generalist, Evelyn seems to have lacked important gifts: we have seen fit to criticize him for not developing an adequate philosophy of Nature, for making himself too available, for an inability to commit himself wholly to one world or another, for responding to the more obvious kinds of display, and for a tendency to dominate his intimates. Not every man, of course, is required to be a philosopher, and it is no doubt a good deal easier for us to see what was happening in Evelyn's world than it was for him. Nor is it entirely fair to force Evelyn into competition with the great or the very greatly talented in other ages. But by all the writing he did, he exposed himself to our questions and laid bare those many places where he only came close to applying his genuine abilities to his world and its needs. Had Evelyn managed to acquire first-rate theoretical knowledge in any one of the many developing fields that interested him; had he possessed the power of a Thoreau to find in Nature a platform from which to dissect his society to its roots; had he been able to combine, as Ruskin did, a highly developed response to beauty and a genuine sense of social indignation—had he succeeded in any of these things —Evelyn would have been a man for the ages. But instead he stands approvingly at the beginning of "the Western absorption in conquering and gaining power over nature"—a conquest that has resulted "not only in the estrangement of man from nature but also indirectly in the estrangement of man from himself." [32] So Evelyn remains a talented amateur, a beloved planter of colewort, a man of fascinating concerns but also a figure too dim in his perceptions of the new world that was being born, a man whose very talents make us wish he had been something more than he was.

The genesis of Burton's *Anatomy of Melancholy*

2

Similarities between John Evelyn and Robert Burton make it possible to put them side by side: both men were profoundly aware of the breadth and complexity of the world in which they lived; both were concerned over the social, economic, and political problems of their age; both loved the past, whether they came to it through rural life or through books; both wrote extensively in an effort to bring the wisdom of the past to bear upon the problems of the present. But the differences are more striking. Evelyn walks casually through gracious palaces and gardens; Burton scowls monkishly at his world, mingling very little sympathy with his general contempt. Burton traveled only through the maps in his library, but he seems to have seen more than Evelyn did in all his years of sight-seeing on the Continent. Burton's lifelong concentration on a single book was a continuing exercise in clarification, definition, and enrichment; it frees him completely from those charges of dilettantism that are so readily leveled against Evelyn. Both men knew diversity, but Burton alone found the power that comes when one reduces the teeming chaos of life to a single grand issue and learns to see it from a single point of view.

This chapter concerns the lifelong effort of Burton to achieve just such a singleness of vision—to organize all that he knew into a pattern that would prove useful for his age and meaningful for himself. The achievement of a point of view can be a tremendous step toward creative activity, for it makes possible that release of human powers which comes when masses of material are organized into relevant patterns, when unnecessary facts are eliminated, and when one's vision is focused on specific details in the sharpest possible way. Few men, however, learn to use this important tool: all too frequently a set of automatic emotional responses serves as a substitute, or some large generalization is developed without any experiential basis, or qualifications are allowed to accumulate haphazardly around an opinion that should be discarded. Edward Reynolds, a contemporary of Robert Burton and a fellow clergyman-psychologist, equated opinion with uncertainty,[1] and the results achieved by people with opinions on many things are rarely very impressive. The distinction between opinion and viewpoint may be an obvious one, but it uncovers a legitimate problem faced by thoughtful men in the 17th century—how to organize all the new facts that were clamoring to be used, how to reduce a vast cultural revolution to personal terms. Burton's response to this challenge is an interesting and instructive one.

Burton was clearly unimpressed by the kind of responses his contemporaries were making, for he describes scholars as apothecaries who "make new mixtures every day" and pick flowers for their own "sterill plots." [2] Burton took a lifetime to complete his mixture, and into it went a fantastic array of data. "I hear new news every day," he laments,

> and those ordinary rumours of war, plagues, fires, inundations, thefts, murders, massacres, meteors, comets, spectrums, prodigies, apparitions, of towns taken, cities besieged in *France, Germany, Turkey, Persia, Poland, &c.* daily musters and preparations, and such like, which these tempestuous times afford, battles fought, so many men slain, monomachies, shipwrecks, piracies, and sea-fights, peace, leagues, stratagems, and fresh alarms. A vast confusion of vows, wishes, actions, edicts, petitions, lawsuits, pleas, laws, proclamations, complaints, grievances, are daily brought to our ears.[3]

Evelyn, apparently also aware of the incalculable diversity of possibilities opening up to modern man, seems to have been insulated from the full impact of what he saw by a certain insensitivity, a lack of mental alertness which dogged him at every stage of his career. Diversity, too, had been the experience of Montaigne: in his essay "Of Experience" he describes the myriad differences—theological, semantic, legal —which men create within every situation. Evelyn's response was one that might be expected from a moderately alert man in an age that was changing too rapidly: he is puzzled, he shoots off in all directions, he dissipates his powers. Montaigne, faithful to the sceptical spirit of the born essayist, finds satisfaction in the most unstable conditions and slowly

evolves a point of view which accepts diversity and impermanence as fundamental facts of life. The Frenchman fairly
revels in the experience of working from several different
centers, having always something more to do, some new attitude to savor.

Burton's experience with the diversity of the world and his
attempt to find a pattern within which he could function was,
in the final analysis, not as successful as Montaigne's. Intellectually more alert than Evelyn, perhaps more intense than
Montaigne, Burton lacked the former's ability to communicate with people and the latter's willingness to let affairs take
their own natural course. Driven by virtually compulsive
needs, he found the world of books and ideas fascinating but
frequently irrelevant, the world of men badly in need of help
but intractable, the fields of medicine and mental health
fascinating but not a little embarrassing. Wrathful against
those who write before seeing their subject clearly ("out of
an itching humour"—Preface, p. 7), he wrote or scribbled
himself, charming many but convincing few that his was an
adequate way to view man's plight. He seems to have contemplated the result with mingled delight and despair:
"When the matter is divers and confused, how should it
otherwise be, but that the Species should be divers and confused?" (I, 52).

I. Burton confronts diversity

The career which Burton chose gave him the fullest possible
view of the contradictions and confusions of the world—but
all too little help in making sense of it. In his famous study

of the Renaissance in Italy, Jacob Burckhardt suggests vividly how hostile to normal human life the career of the humanist was, involving as it did exhausting lectureships, tutorships, and secretaryships, lacking roots and any fundamental morality, and very often making marriage and a settled life impossible. From such problems, Burckhardt observes, only the strongest could escape unscathed. Burton was, of course, no wandering scholar. The benefices which he held shielded him from many of the pressures to which earlier humanists had been subject, and the rules of his college were strict enough to regulate his life within a fairly rigid framework. The frustrations he faced were of a more subtle kind, involving nothing less than gnawing questions about the ultimate value of the career which he had chosen and deep distress about the isolation in which he lived. I have little doubt that on more than one occasion he felt what Don Quixote felt as he was lowered into the Cave of Montesinos: "already weary of hanging by the loins, discouraged by the profound darkness of the region below me, destitute of a guide, and not knowing whither I went." [4] Bergen Evans thinks that Burton hated university life. A more recent student, Lawrence Babb, hedges, suggesting that Burton disliked the pedantry but found much by way of compensation. Gerth and Mills, discussing the problem of motive-mongering and self-doubt, suggest that "institutionally marginal persons" (such as Burton was in part) are especially susceptible to confusion and self-questioning. Burton himself, as we shall see, makes contradictory statements. [5]

According to his own testimony, Burton was born of honorable parents and an ancient family and was educated at Sutton Coldfield, Warwickshire, where he grew up. Despite

the praise which he has for his family, Bergen Evans thinks
that Burton regarded his mother as unaffectionate and believed that he had had his feelings badly hurt in childhood.[6]
Whatever the experience was, it left its mark in Burton's
response to the way children suffer at the hands of parents
and teachers, and it did not help to push the boy into any
positive and effective contact with his world. Anthony Wood
observes that Burton made "considerable progress in logic
and philosophy" at Brasenose College, Oxford, later becoming interested in such curious things as mathematics, the cal-
culation of nativities, land surveying, and philology. Both
Paul Jordan-Smith and Lawrence Babb have expanded this
hint about Burton's learning, describing in detail his knowledge of medicine, psychology, the supernatural, religion, and
mathematics.[7] Such wide reading explains Wood's observation that Burton was fond of "interlarding his common discourses among them with verses from the poets or sentences
from classical authors." [8] But a good deal of this learning
Burton amassed late in his career, for the training which
both Oxford and Cambridge offered was almost exclusively
philosophical and logical.[9] Burton took his undergraduate
studies at Brasenose and was a divinity student at Christ
Church. He received his B.A. in 1602 and his B.D. in 1614,
and he became Vicar of St. Thomas's, Oxford, in 1616. One
event from the earlier part of his career which seems to have
influenced his later outlook (specifically his sense of resentment and rejection) was his apparent failure to achieve a
much desired church appointment. This may have happened
before 1614 or between 1614 and 1616, and it is never specifically identified. But the problem of preferment comes up
so frequently in the literature of the period that one is forced

to assume that it marked a crucial step in the career of a young scholar. With the appointment, a degree of success and influence was virtually assured; without it, nothing but struggle, frustration, and the isolation of a rural parish lay ahead. Burton won further benefices in 1624 and 1632, but these were never able to offset the sense of incompetence he felt because he was passed over in the middle of the second decade of the century; consequently this complaint becomes a permanent part of his book:

Preferment I could never get, although my friendes providence, care, alacritie and bounty was never wanting to doe me good, yet either through mine owne default, infelicity, want or neglect of opportunity, or iniquitie of times, preposterous proceeding, mine hopes were still frustrate, and I left behind, as a Dolphin on shore, confined to my Colledge, as *Diogenes* to his tubbe (page 4).

Burton was later to admit that eventually he stopped bustling about in search of advancement, and he even grants that he has had noble benefactors. But the pains of early disappointment continued to be felt, for in later editions of the *Anatomy* he includes a story about just such a situation as he must have known. This is the poignant and quixotic story of the vacant benefice. The living is sought by men of wealth, scholarship, religious zeal, and by men united to the church by ties of blood, marriage, and friendship. In despair at having to choose between so many worthy contenders the puzzled bishop finally awards the prebendary to a poor but worthy student with hardly any claim at all upon it. "But alas!" laments Burton, "it is but a tale, a mere fiction, 'twas never so, never like to be." [10] Ultimately this experience seems to have driven Burton to the shoulder-shrugging mood

of Heraclitus, whose philosophy he sums up in a curt "so things go round, ebb and flow," and to the cynicism of Democritus, who ascribed the world to chance, as Dante observes. Thus Burton adapted himself, with greater or lesser resentment, to a "silent, sedentary, solitary, private life, *mihi & musis,* in the University" (Preface, p. 3), outwardly quiet but inwardly the victim of considerable mental distress.

From *The Anatomy of Melancholy* itself we get a profounder and more comprehensive—if also somewhat muddied —view of Burton's attempt to shape all the diversity which confronted him into some consistent and viable point of view. My argument requires at this point some examination of the way Burton undertook this process—admittedly a task that will demand some deductions where there are no clear facts. Between 1621 and 1651, when a sixth, posthumous edition was published, Burton expanded his original book (of some 860 pages) by the addition of a third more material. In this expansion there lies abundant material for textual study, though the sheer bulk of the material has frustrated various attempts to publish (if not to prepare) a much needed variorum edition. Certain passages like the Utopia and the section on Love Melancholy have been examined, however, and a study of the changes in the second edition has been completed. All the changes which were made suggest that the text, even when it was set down on paper, was in a very fluid state, as to details, but firmly established in its fundamental patterns. Having chosen melancholy as his focus, Burton found himself the prisoner of his subject, unable to make alterations except by minute or massive additions here and there. These post-publication

changes suggest that even vaster alterations must have been the rule during the "chaos of preordination" which preceded publication of the first edition. In the years before 1621 Burton evidently amassed more and more material and chopped, expanded, or otherwise altered it to fit a theme that was constantly growing sharper and more demanding. When did the collection of data begin? What passages were composed first? When did Burton finally decide that melancholy should be his point of view? These are questions for which there are no definite answers. But some intelligent guesses can be made—guesses that may be helpful in assessing the way Burton's ever deepening comprehension of his world assumed shape and coherence.

Speculative as the study of literary genetics may be, it nonetheless seems that some important things about a writer's personality can be learned by studying the way he works. Unfortunately the kind of materials that are useful for such an examination—early notes, rough drafts, sheets of revisions—are, for the present case, not available or at least identifiable as such. Unlike many of his contemporaries, Burton left no commonplace book and no record of his literary plans, so that the earliest observations we have are those that appear in the preface to the first edition. The fact that Burton wrote in prose creates still other difficulties, for the sheer massiveness of the text invalidates the kind of minute textual study to which poetry lends itself so well. What we have to go on, first of all, is the text of the original edition and the evidence of manuscript changes that it supplies, the changes (primarily of additional material) that Burton made in succeeding editions; and, third, the internal evidence supplied by the various inconsistencies and contra-

dictions in the text, by the presence of a great variety of literary forms and ideas, and by the outline, the preface, and the digressions. One assumption is absolutely fundamental, and this is that the *Anatomy* was not produced *seriatim*, as it stands in the first edition, but rather that chunks of essentially unrelated material were composed at different times (or at least gathered together under unifying headings in a commonplace book), and that these chunks of material reflect Burton's developing and changing interests, his constant readjustments of point of view. Not until a great deal of reading and note-taking and a great deal of casual writing had been done was a large book on melancholy conceived, planned, and written.

There is perhaps a good deal in this statement that will be obvious to the careful reader of the *Anatomy,* and on *a priori* grounds—Burton's general carelessness with his text, the diversity of his experience, and what is known about the composition of other Renaissance books—all provide support for this argument. Modern studies of the composition of *The Faerie Queene,* Calvin's *Institutes of the Christian Religion,* Montaigne's *Essays,* and Hooker's *Ecclesiastical Polity* suggest that the process of composition in the Renaissance could be a very chaotic affair indeed, with books at their inception resembling only faintly the ultimate product. Few would argue that Burton's mind was more orderly than Calvin's, or Spenser's or Hooker's. My feeling about the composition of the *Anatomy* received some support from Babb's judgment that the book as it stands is not quite the book which Burton set out to write, but that in it a purpose was superimposed upon a purpose.[11] If my premise can be accepted, we can undertake to examine the state of the fin-

ished book, how the book may have developed
development reflected Burton's shifting and emerging
point, and how Burton tried to organize as much material as
possible into a single work that would somehow reduce the
chaos of the world to a comprehensible entity.

II. The Anatomy of Melancholy: *confusion and order*

Some evidence for the kind of process I have in mind is
clearly demanded—evidence that would point, first of all, to
a considerable lapse of time during composition as well as to
some uncertainty about the ultimate goal. Burton confesses
that his manuscript went unrevised to the printer's, after he
had "licked" it into shape much as a bear was thought to
form her newborn cubs; he points to frequent changes in
style as evidence of the remissness with which he treated his
material; and he says that the book was "confusedly tum-
bled out: without art, invention, judgement, witte, learning,
harsh, absurd, insolent, indiscreet, ill-composed, vaine, scur-
rile . . ." (page 9).[12] There are, it must be admitted, some
indications that this pose of carelessness was, to at least a
degree, assumed and that frequently Burton was in complete
control of his work. Thus on occasion he points out, like any
careful writer, what he has done or is about to do; more than
once he numbers his main points in an argument or analysis;
frequently he indicates painstakingly the relationship of one
minor topic to the whole problem of melancholy. And while
much of his material is not essentially relevant to the problem of mental health, his analysis of specific topics is frequently keen and detailed. But such evidences of planning

be balanced against contrary evidence—evidence of lack of direction or control. Such loss of focus is apparent, for instance, as Burton abandons the care and objectivity with which he discusses the ideal state for an ill-conceived and badly organized diatribe against the people who inhabit it. It is not unusual to see him going back over material he has already treated fully, or retelling the same anecdote after a few pages. Frequently he catches himself with a "This is not the matter in hand" (page 554) or "But hoo? I am now gone quite out of sight, I am almost giddy with roving about" (page 300), and at the end of the Preface he is clearly much concerned about "overshooting" himself. His confession on page six of the first edition, "When I first tooke this taske in hand," seems to suggest a much longer lapse of time than would normally occur in the writing of so few pages; and there is at the end of the Preface an even more remarkable confession: "Although for these above named reasons, I had a just cause to undertake this subject . . . I have a more serious intent at this time" (Preface, page 69). Here, it would seem, a gap of several months or even years is indicated. Instances like these cast the burden of proof upon those inclined to argue that Burton chose his subject, gathered his material in an orderly manner, made an outline, and proceeded to write his book.

Also suggestive of an underlying disunity in Burton's book are the numerous changes of mood and attitude which he records. I am not referring to the superficial, obviously intentional changes that are outlined in the "Abstract of Melancholy," where Burton describes the disease which is his subject as sweet and then as damned, or to those skittish alterations about tobacco, which is praised as divine, rare,

superexcellent, and then condemned as hellish, devilish, and damned (page 453). Much more fundamental are the diverse views he appears to have held about his career. The lonely scholar of Burton's day was at the mercy of ignorant patrons who made the most insulting demands on those whom they supported. It was not unusual for a scholar to be more poorly paid than a laborer; there was no tenure; ecclesiastical posts were frequenty isolated in wretched villages far from books or conversation. Nevertheless, at one time Burton was convinced of the absolute supremacy of the scholarly life. He notes the enthusiasm with which King James visited the Oxford libraries, and he speaks with a sense of genuine dedication about his own career:

Such is the excellency of those studies, that al those ornaments and bubbles of wealth are not worthy to be compared to them, *crede mihi* (saith one) *extingui dulce erit Mathematicarum artium studio,* I could even live and dye with those studies, and take more pleasure, true content of mind in them, then thou dost in all thy wealth, how rich soever thou art (page 352).

Something of this enthusiasm about books always remains glittering before Burton even though at other times he observes bitterly that

. . . after all their paines taken in the *Universities,* coste & charge, expences, irksome houres, laborious taskes, wearisome dayes, dangers, hazards, barred *interim* from all pleasures, which other men have, mewed up like hawkes all their lives, if they chance to wade through them, they shall in the end be rejected and contemned, and which is their greatest misery, driven to their shifts, exposed to want, poverty and beggery (page 172).

An even more fundamental shift of viewpoint is to be seen in the changes in Burton's attitude toward mankind. On one page he seems another scoffing Lucian, convinced that the human race is hopelessly doomed to folly and incapable of redemption; a few pages later he speaks out for the orthodox Christian view that man is both animal and a little lower than the angels. In general the mood of the Preface is highly critical, bitterly sceptical, hardly compatible with a spirit of Christian charity, manic in instability. Thus lawyers are condemned as

A purse-milking nation, a clamorous company, gowned vulters, theeves, & Seminaries of discord, that take upon them to make peace, but are indeed the very disturbers of our peace, a company of irreligious Harpyes, scraping, griping Catchpoles (Preface, page 48).

When Burton's angry fit is upon him, there is no area of human life that escapes his lashing tongue: even his references to religious matters are limited to caustic remarks about the overabundance of sermons and unworthy saints, the vagaries of hermits, or the treachery of the Jesuits. The Bible is quoted, but chiefly as a proof of human folly—for which Aristophanes would have served just as well. Compare, on the other hand, a passage like this from the First Partition, which follows Burton's confession of his own folly in seeking to anatomize the world:

The impulsive cause of all these miseries in man, this privation or destruction of Gods Image, the cause of death and diseases, of all temporall and eternall punishments, was the sinne of our first parent *Adam,* in eating of the forbidden fruit, by the Divells instigation and allurement. His disobedience, pride, ambition, in-

temperance, incredulity, curiosity, from whence proceeded orig-
inall sinne, & that generall corruption of mankinde, as from a
fountaine flowed all bad inclinations, and actuall transgressions,
which cause our several calamities, inflicted upon us for our sinnes
(page 2).

We find statements not unlike this in Hobbes, who was fundamentally a most irreligious man, and they do not destroy
our sense of his hostility to the Biblical view of things. But
so sincere is the religious feeling that Burton elsewhere
evinces that we are forced to take this as an analysis of the
human situation from a man who was at heart a Christian in
his sympathies. In any case, the difference between the two
passages is as fundamental as that between St. Paul or
Augustine, on the one hand, and Aretino or Rabelais, on the
other.

No area of Burton's concern is fuller of shifts and sudden
changes than his treatment of love, a subject he was to describe eventually as a "Tragi-Comedy" [13] and as a "bottom-
less pit." He obviously shared Ovid's feeling that the game
of love was dominated above all else by changes, fickleness,
mixed failures and successes, and he made maximum use of
this point of view. Thus Burton can at one moment describe
glowingly the joy of happy, conjugal love, and, two pages
later, the way marriage is ruined by "women's unnatural,
unsatiable lust." [14]

'Tis so with us Bachelors, when we see and behold those sweet
faces, those gaudy shews that women make, observe their pleasant
gestures and graces, give ear to their Siren tunes, see them dance,
&c., we think their conditions are as fine as their faces, we are
taken with dumb signs, *in amplexum ruimus*, we rave, we burn,
and would fain be married. But when we feel the miseries, cares,

woes, that accompany it, we make our moan many of us, cry out at length, and cannot be released.[15]

In its diversity, Burton's treatment of love embraces reasons (affability, kindness, consanguinity), as well as symptoms (blushing, heaviness, rapid pulse, and generosity). Love may, he suggests, produce valuable changes in the personality, making a *"hard base untractable Churle . . . facile, gentle, and easie to be intreated"* (page 620), or it may lead to a complete loss of values. Its irrational, appetitive aspects make it light, fantastical, wanton, rash, and lascivious; but it can be rational, too, as in marriage, or when it stems from affection for virtue or for one's country. So light as to be stirred by kissing, it also has the power to bind together the entire cosmos. Some of the conflicting views Burton records are doubtless implicit in his subject and no blame is chargeable to him. But on a deeper level a fundamental indecisiveness is apparent, a mercurial shifting and turning that neatly sums up the shifts and turns of the whole book.

His inability to sustain a single point of view on even his basic problems was not the only difficulty Burton faced in composing the *Anatomy*. Another problem lay in Burton's inability to sustain a steady degree of interest in his material. He was apparently aware that much of what he had written was wretched hackwork, for he speaks of it as a "confused lump" and as "warmed-over cabbage," and he apologizes for having written "in an extemporanean stile . . . *stans pede in uno,* as hee made verses, out of a confused company of notes" (unpaged conclusion to the first edition). So it is that any discussion of Burton's style is complicated by Burton's ability to produce passages of genuine beauty and interest and by a carelessness which lured him into page after page of wretched hackwork. No doubt Burton was hurried on many occasions, but there were other times when he labored with no other purpose than to fill in points in his outline. Then he produced prose like this:

> Outwardly taken to expell windes, are oyles, as of Camomile, Rue, Bayes, &c. fomentations of the hypochondries, with the decoctions of Dill, Penneriall, Rue, Bay leaves, cummin, &c., bagges of Camomile Flowers, Anniseed, Cummin, Bayes, Rue, Wormwood, oyntments of the oyle of Spinkenard, Wormwood, Rue &c., *Areteus* prescribes Cataplasmes of Camomile Flowres, Fennell, Anniseeds, Cummin, Rosemary, Wormwood leaves, &c. (page 486).

Equally bleak passages occur when Burton discusses the six nonnatural things and the perturbations (Partition I), unlawful cures and purges (Partition II), and love philtres (Partition III). In these patchwork sections a mass of notes is presented—material not adequately digested, weighed, or arranged. An almost certain indication that Burton is working directly from notes is his habit of beginning sentence after sentence, paragraph after paragraph by citing the author or the title of his source. When he has taken the time to think about his material and let his imagination play upon it, source references are eliminated or move to less conspicuous parts of his sentences. There is a heavy concentration of dull passages in the medical sections, and this may suggest a fundamental distaste on Burton's part for much of the material to which he had committed himself. The fame of his book rests, of course, on those sections that seem to gather up all the richness of Renaissance experience, all the intensity of Burton's own response to life. Such passages as that on the rectification of air, on exercise, on erotic love (enriched with his wide reading in the Latin and English poets) reflect a total involvement of Burton's personality with his material and offer proof of the work of a creative mind. Burton's power to sustain his inspiration, however, was limited.

Another evidence of the complexity of the process of composition through which the *Anatomy* passed can be seen in the incredible variety of literary forms and themes which Burton presents. In this single book there are essays, sermons, catalogues, pasquinades, anecdotes, maxims, characters, parodies, panegyrics, complaints, and consolations—and the list is just beginning. In many cases a paragraph or a brace of pages has a finish and polish that contrasts vividly with the carelessness of the book as a whole. Burton's skill lay obviously in the smaller forms, which could be embedded in larger, unshaped masses of material. Narrative is a good example: Burton handles the brief, semi-oral anecdote effectively but does a poorer job with material that might have made a novella or a romance. He was a skilled essayist and writer of sermons, and in these genres he achieves that degree of finish and coherence that seems to lie at the heart of our sense of form.

Of control and polish there is ample in Burton's discussion of poverty and want as causes of melancholy (page 202). Beginning with the firm thesis that all men have abhorred these conditions, Burton suggests vigorously (but with more coherence than his anger sometimes permits) that we will do anything to avoid them: "We will turne parasites and slaves, prostitute our selves, sweare and lye, damne our bodies and soules" (page 203) in order to escape. He appeals next to experience, dramatizing the way a rich man is treated ("God blesse his good worship, his honor") and describing sensuously his powers and his pleasures. Anecdotes from Renaissance history and a reference to Plutarch are closed out with highly topical allusions to Sir Fastidious Brisk and Sir Petronel Flash. Turning next to the suffering of the poor man, Burton sets forth a series of sordid vignettes of human suffering, closing with a prayer for a contented mind. The literary quality of the entire passage is to be seen in its logical movement, its depth of controlled feeling, the striking absence of the normal torrent of allusions and authorities, and the exceptionally close integration of the anecdotes. The passage lacks the sharp wit of Bacon, the mellowness of Montaigne, but it is nevertheless rational prose of a very high order.

The same sense of coherence can be noted in the description of the ideal state which Burton included in his Democritus Junior preface (page 56 ff.), where he moves unerringly through a large and complex amount of material. Beginning with an apology for dealing with social problems, Burton follows the lead of More and turns first to matters of geography, the organization of the kingdom, the size and location of its cities, and the establishment of markets, houses, harbors, and hospitals. He moves then to the field of economics, speaking out against monopolies and urging intensive use of every available acre of ground. He concludes with a thoughtful treatment of such issues as the function of the nobility, the form of government, foreign relations, crafts and trades, legal problems, civil punishments, marriage, and the conduct of families. At this point, however, his power to protect the material from his own impatience slips away, and he begins once again to rail at human folly. Nevertheless, this passage achieves a remarkable harmony of style, structure, and content, and provides a striking revelation of the personality behind the pen. If More emerges from his Utopia as a genial and charitable Christian socialist, Burton strikes the reader as decidedly cynical and pragmatic, fond of his role as a detached observer, obsessed with the shortcomings of his age, but nonetheless a man of sympathy, wide interests, and rich background.

Other passages in the *Anatomy* achieve much the same coherence, though one hears little about them since they are buried deep in Burton's vast store of words: the digression on spirits in Partition I; the essays in Partition II on water, geography, national differences, weather, cosmology, life and soil, sports, air, and the long section on Stoicism. Something of a gem is the little sermon on repentance which Burton added after 1621, a masterpiece of homiletic form complete down to the traditional parts—consideration of the text, division of the subject, amplification, explanation, and application, with rich language and rhetorical figures to embellish the whole. The passage no more resembles most of Burton than the sermons of Sterne resemble *Tristram Shandy*.

But moments of mellow coherence or deep religious feeling cannot long mask the fundamental mood of raillery and satire which finds its natural vehicle in a numer of forms common in Burton—among them the catalogue, the "jeremiad," and the anecdote. Mere listing is not necessarily a satiric or an ironic method of presenting material (Whitman uses this device to suggest the abundance of goodness in the world), for the satiric overtones emerge only when a great many good and bad things are heaped together meaninglessly in what rhetoricians call "congeries." Behind the list or catalogue as Burton employs it lies the suggestion that man viewed *en masse* can never be more than a wretched impossibility, that the world is too diverse, too wicked to cope with: "To insist in all particulars, were an *Herculean* taske, to reckon up . . . mad labours, endevours, carriages, ridiculous actions, gestures . . . madnesse of villages, hypocrisie, inconstancy &c. braules, contentions, would aske an expert *Vesalius* to anatomise every member (Preface, page 67). Much of Burton's bitterness is conveyed by what might best be called sniping: man is up one day and down the next; he "bangles" away his best hours; he will stop at nothing to gain his ends; and it is hard to know whether to laugh or to weep. But on some occasions Burton winds himself up to a pitch of sustained invective and produces passages which by their very rashness and intemperance approach the sublime. Such is the liturgy to the damned in the Preface: How Democritus would have laughed, Burton writes, "To see a man turne himselfe into all shapes like a Camelion . . . to act twenty parts at once for his advantage . . . to see a man protest friendship, kisse his hand, smile with an intent to do mischief. . . . To see men wholy led by affection . . . to see a man to wear his braines in his belly" (Preface, pp. 33–4). A similar litany, constructed out of a series of moral impossibilities based on "if" was to appear in later editions in the section on discontents in Partition Two.

One of the chief characteristics of pre-Restoration prose is an abundance of rich, sometimes satiric or cynical, sometimes highly sophisticated anecdote, often borrowed from classical sources. In *The Anatomy of Melancholy* the clever tale comes as close as any literary genre can to being the peculiar vehicle of Burton's personal vision of life. Indeed, his effectiveness with the form is somewhat diminished by his prodigal use of it, as well as by his lack of skill as a raconteur. His habit of telling six stories where one would do makes his book discursive and deprives any single story of any organic quality. Nevertheless, his own enthusiasm for the great tales from the European ocean of story is infectious (*"I never read that place of Panthea in Xenephon but I am as much affected as if I were present with her"*—page 549), and his versions of the old tales, peculiar as they may be, are one of the chief and most characteristic pleasures afforded by his book.

Frequently, Burton does little more than allude to stories which he thought, apparently, that all his readers would know. Verstegan's account of the Pied Piper is, more thanks to Browning than to Burton ("The Divell, in the likeness of a pied piper, carried away 130. children"—page 68), one of the most popular of all folk tales. Burton is similarly indebted to Laurence Sterne and John Keats for amplifying the bare bones which he presented. Some anecdotes, like many that had already been told by Cervantes, are scarcely more than medical or psychiatric case histories, with little or no literary merit. To point out the peculiarities of scholars, Burton tells how Aquinas, standing before Lewis of France, forgot the business at hand and blurted out an attack on the Manichees (page 171). Jealousy is illustrated in the story of the young scholar more interested in his books than in his wife who, noting one day her interest in other men, at length "began to suspect, and turne a little yellow, aswel he might" (page 674). Many anecdotes are relegated to insignificant parentheses or to subordinate clauses, or they become hopelessly involved in the telling:

But as the Oxe, tired, told the Camel, (both serving one master)
that refused to carry some part of his burden, before it were long
he should be compelled to carry all his packe, and his skinne to
boot (which by and by the Oxe being dead fell out) (page 356).

Many old stories attracted Burton because they pointed up
the grossness and stupidity of life and thus served as vehicles
for his own bitterness and outrage. The familiar story of the
Widow of Ephesus, who was seduced by a soldier while she
guarded her late husband's tomb, is such a tale, and Burton
tells it twice. Similar stories deal with a storm-tossed Syra-
cusan who threw his wife overboard with his other heavy
baggage *"quia maximum pondus erat"* (page 647) and with
the Jew who drowned in a sewer because his fellows would
not rescue him on Saturday, or the Christians, on Sunday.
Stories designed to suggest the foolish indifference of men to
values are those of the fool who sold a mouse for two hundred pence during a famine—only to die himself of starva-
tion; and of the madman who questioned a rich hunter about
the value of hawks he caught with his very expensive equipment. Weak as art, Burton's stories nevertheless suggest in
all their wonderful diversity of mood and matter the teeming
variety of the world which the anatomist was seeking to
comprehend.

One step beyond the anecdote the Renaissance distilled the
wisdom and vision of the ancients into that quintessence of
experience, the pithy and witty aphorism. Once again, the
unfocused, untamed view which Burton took of his world
is to be seen in the torrential, tumble-down-Dick manner in
which he sprays out proverbs, some in Latin, some in English; some worldly, some homely; some too loose-jointed to
be memorable, others noteworthy for their almost Baconian
balance. Burton seems to have taken special delight in this

form in his discussion of "Remedies of Discontents," where he calls on Horace, Lucretius, Lucan, Jerome, Chrysostom, Seneca, Augustine, and Lipsius to outdo even Polonius or the best efforts of Cervantes' "eternal proverb-swilling swag belly" Panza:

Know thyself. Be contented with thy lot. Trust not wealth, beauty nor parasites, they will bring thee to destruction. Have peace with all men, warre with vice. Be not idle. Looke before you leap. Beware of Had I wist . . . (page 427).

Human experience will not be crammed into such brief compass: to try is either to reveal one's superficiality or to make the gesture of throwing up one's hands in despair. Burton, a man of great depth, would seem to be doing the latter. Here is virtuosity, but of a bastard kind, a kind more vendible in some farmers' almanac than in a treatise on Neo-Stoicism.

The *character* was a form to which Burton turned with pleasure, his material, his interest in human behavior, his cynicism, and his concern with mental aberration being what they were. But these very interests led him also to ignore completely many subjects described by his contemporaries—Overbury, Earle, and Hall. There are in Burton very few descriptions of human virtue, or of such normal categories as trades, professions, national types, or institutions which were popular subjects. Yet references to Theophrastus and to Joseph Hall, the pioneer English character writer, indicate that Burton knew well what was going on in this genre. Burton, however, lacked art, and his long-standing habit of introspection hindered rather than helped: the form in its perfection demands an absolutely objective analysis of a clearly distinguishable human type. At their worst, the Burtonian characters are indictments rather than objective descriptions—and indictments of very traditional subjects at that. Burton's discussions of the henpecked husband or the lovesick beau are frequently marred by literary allusions or moral commentary, and his indictments of social types like the gamester or the newly rich suffer from too much anger and too little structure. On the other hand descriptions like this one (of hypochondriacs) show real dramatic flair: "If their finger doe but ake [they] run, ride, send for a Physitian, as many Gentlewomen frequently doe; and when he comes, they make it worse than it is, by amplifying that which is not" (page 301). This passage suggests that Burton frequently concentrates upon external behavior, differing fundamentally in this respect from Hall, whose sketches often show deep understanding of human motives. Thus while Burton describes the covetous man as "a perpetuall drudge . . . a slave, a wretch, a dustworm" (page 155), Hall shows how the same man,

when his guests are parted, talkes how much every man devoured, and how many cups were emptied, and feeds his family with the mouldy remnants a moneth after. If his servant breake but an earthen dish for want of light, he abates it out of his quarters wages.[16]

Overbury's definition of the character as "wit's descant on any plain song" points up the basic deficiencies of Burton's work: he has forsaken Theophrastian mildness and the mental ingenuity of his contemporaries for a general, caustic indictment of the world in the Jonsonian tradition. The neatness of phrase which characterizes the work of Fuller and Hall is particularly missed in the opening definition and the conceited *adieu*. Without this artistry, the character itself tends to be absorbed into the amorphous mass of Burton's prose. Finally, Burton's characters reveal deficiencies often noted in the work of academic psychologists as contrasted with the work of the novelist or playwright—an accumulation of data which obscures the meaning of the facts, failure to see the human being as a whole, a neglect of the art which would provide focus and coherence. Burton's work in this genre suggests again the trouble he had with a point of view and confirms that truism of character-criticism that all the best characters are in character books.

III. The Anatomy of Melancholy: *the process of composition*

To sumarize: *The Anatomy of Melancholy* is made up of a great variety of literary genres and conflicting viewpoints—two elements which suggest a long period of experimentation on Burton's part and considerable uncertainty as to where his scholarship, his literary dabblings, and his observations on human life were taking him. The same tumbling abundance can be seen in the great variety of subjects which Burton discusses at one time or another in his book. Other books on melancholy which were being written when Burton worked were relatively limited in scope: the effects of melancholy on body and soul, the causal agents (God and Nature), the natural and unnatural forms of the disease, the problem of body-soul relations, and the effects of the disease upon the personality. All these subjects and more are encompassed in the enormous scope of Burton's work—the nature of the ideal state, the peculiar vices of the English, problems of law and church, human anatomy, the operation of spirits, astrology, the sufferings of scholars, the problem of poverty, the difficulties of nuns and widows, ideal building sites, the joys of chess, the effect of beauty upon the male, the problem of marriage, the psychology of jealousy. Burton obviously knew the English situation thoroughly. But at the same time he evidently experienced some confusion about his purpose or the area upon which he should concentrate. When for the first time he put down his notes on ecology, he was probably writing as a Renaissance humanist, well acquainted with Greek theories on the effect of the land on human well-being, with little thought that he might someday anatomize melancholy. We can see from our vantage point how each of these interests led ultimately to melancholy, but we must not assume that the direction was always quite so clear to Burton.

It would seem, then, that at some time in his career (he says that it was after being penned up in the University for over twenty years—page 3), Burton had amassed a collection of generally unrelated essays on curious problems or —at least—a commonplace book filled with notes from his voracious reading, his prying mind, his "roving humor," and his desire for "some smattering in all" (page 3). This was a moment when he apparently confronted his material with the same sense of helplessness that Laurence Sterne describes in *Tristram Shandy,* having

> Accounts to reconcile:
> Anecdotes to pick up:
> Inscriptions to make out:
> Stories to weave in:
> Traditions to sift:
> Personages to call upon:

> Panegyricks to paste up at this door:
> Pasquinades at that. . . .

What direction was Burton to take through all this material? In the books of many of his contemporaries we can see some possibilities, as well as clear reasons why Burton did not make this choice or that. Erasmus, a figure who resembles Burton in many ways, appears to have collected similar material and to have explored similar possibilities. Both were marginal churchmen who strike us—or struck their contemporaries—as putting perhaps too high a value on neutrality, who never comitted themselves to any single point of view except the age-old humanistic tradition, who tried persistently and with greater or lesser success to apply their learning to the problems of suffering humanity. Many of the subjects treated by Erasmus in his familiar colloquies parallel subjects which Burton treats—a fact which suggests that Burton's book, too, might have taken the form of a series of dialogues, sometimes critical or satirical, sometimes affirmative and constructive, always witty. Both writers discuss benefice hunting, the horrors of war, spirits, marriage, liars, vices, doctors, public life, envy and jealousy, the operations of "horse-traders," religious pilgrimages, casuistry, grammarians, and the wickedness of monks—and they do it in a chatty, informal way with none of the careful organization or pretentiousness of writers of "treatises." Lawrence Babb suggests that Erasmus's *Praise of Folly* may have influenced Burton, and it is plain that there are elements of both "fool" literature and the *encomium* in the *Anatomy*.[17] Professor Hoyt Hudson notes that a kind of rhetorical game grew up over the eulogy, with the goal being to praise anything, no matter how unworthy. He traces the tradition back to Sebastian Brant and his *Ship of Fools,* where the author, having found a convenient container, tried to cram into it as many kinds of human stupidity as he could find.[18] Burton followed these patterns only incidentally: the cynicism was there, but along with it a much greater fund of technical knowledge than these forms demanded as well as a deep-rooted desire to be useful, to contribute to the alleviation of human misery, to promote understanding and sympathy.

The Baconian essay provided another path which Burton might have followed, for the subjects about which Bacon wrote fit very well into the general structure of melancholy. The essays on death, revenge, adversity, parents, marriage and the single life, envy, love, great place, atheism, superstition, delays, expense, suspicion, fortune, deformity, anger, vicissitude, and vainglory (Burton's φιλαμτία) all deal with subjects which Burton was to identify as causes of mental depression. Some of these same essays, and others as well— those on love, friendship, travel, youth and age, buildings, studies, and gardens—are concerned with the cure of mental illness or the reconstruction of human life. This sharing of themes by Bacon and Burton is not a superficial matter: Bacon is truly a founder and prince in the Kingdom of Melancholy. But Burton's genius lay in expanding rather than contracting, and he was generally incapable of submitting for long to any severe literary discipline. I suspect, too, that he was considerably more concerned with knowledge than with wisdom, but it is wisdom, primarily, that is the province of the born essayist.

I find other suggestive similarities between Burton and Cervantes' *Don Quixote;* this is especially true of subject

matter (the loss of a normal grip on reality, the establishment of a world view too exclusively on books, and the
search for a new identity through some pseudonym such as
"Democritus" or "Quixote"). Loss of contact with present
reality is suggested by the tendency of both Democritus and
Sancho to resort to proverbs as a way by which (supposedly)
the world might finally be understood and controlled. In
both books there is strong expression of the tension between
the active life and the contemplative: Burton, it has been
noted, has mixed feelings about scholarship, and the Don
feels strongly the merit of arms over letters. The subjectivity
which led Burton to a study of melancholy is to be seen again
in the retirement of the Don to Sierra Morena and in his
visit to the depths of the Cave of Montesinos. And that sense
of frustration, which is so basic a cause of melancholy, has nowhere been better described than by Cervantes in his account
of the sufferings of Don Quixote at the hands of the prisoners
whom he frees from their chains. The Don, Cervantes observes, was "filled with sullen regret, to find himself so bar-
barously used by those whom he had so highly obliged." [19]
Melancholy delusions are frequently described by Burton,
and they have their parallels in the Don's fantasies—Master
Peter's puppet show, the incident of the wineskins, the duel
with the captive lion, the tilt with the windmill, and Dulcinea
del Toboso. Both authors devote considerable time to the
specific forms of melancholy associated with lovers—Cervantes in the long tale of Cardenio and Luscinda; Burton
throughout the entire Third Partition. Both writers suggest
time and again that contact with the word of humble people
is healthy: Burton praises a life that permits enjoyment of
the elemental forces of Nature, and Cervantes counters the

Don's airy delusions with Sancho's peasant realism and sends the squire to Comacho's wedding feast, where fleshly pleasures of every sort abound. And both Burton and Cervantes were concerned with the reconstruction of society: the equivalents of Burton's Utopia are Cervantes' elaborate attacks on lawyers, clergymen, and doctors and his description (to Sancho by way of the Don) of how to govern a kingdom. If Burton possessed more spontaneity of mood than Bacon and a less bridled imagination, he nevertheless lacked the sustained narrative power of Cervantes. Lacking "art," he wisely rejected a fictional narrative as his form—a narrative that would have been overly rigid (loose as the picaresque form may be) and would have made demands upon him in terms of character analysis and development that he could not have met.

It may be that Burton, at one time or another, considered such possibilities and that the outline which he developed was a confession to himself that all but one avenue was closed. This famous outline, which carries painstaking detail to almost ludicrous lengths, has long been regarded as one of the book's scholarly cruxes, with a good deal of the debate centering on how seriously it should be taken. Some older critics (among them the author of the article on Burton in *The Dictionary of National Biography*) have pronounced it a parody on the pedantic and fantastic outlines popular in the late Renaissance. John Ferriar, in a book on Sterne published at the end of the 18th Century, referred to Burton's *archness* in compiling it. William Mueller, on the other hand, regards it more seriously and speaks of the "scrupulous fidelity of Burton's text to the three synopses." [20] That a text should follow a carefully prepared outline is no more than might reasonably be expected; the real difficulty I find to lie in the assumption that Burton composed the outline and then wrote a book to fit it. Had he done so, it is not easy to explain why he should retell the same stories, why his attacks upon human folly are so completely unbridled, why he is not better able to control the changes in his moods, or why, in the Second Partition, he should insert a curious little chapter on the cure of melancholy (which is, after all, about one third of the subject of the entire book). Readers of Sterne take such mercurial shifts for granted, but Burton's elaborate outline indicates that he intended to compose a carefully constructed, analytical book. That he did not prompts the suggestion that he compiled his outline only after he had written a number of completely independent sections, so that his outline fitted the work he had already completed and guided him in finishing the whole book. What forced his hand into a book on melancholy was the development of his interest in medicine and psychology and the realization that in melancholy (seen both medically and metaphorically) he had a subject broad enough to embrace all that he had written—and more. This moment, I am convinced, came very late; Babb notes that the outline may be put at least after 1615.[21] Burton tells us something about why he chose melancholy as his subject. He was, he says, at this time obsessed by laziness and by *gravidum cor*. He suggests, too, that he has got all his knowledge by melancholizing, and it may be that Democritus, who wrote a book on this subject, suggested another to Burton. In any case, melancholy was for Burton like "a rillet . . . deducted from that maine channell of my other studies, in which I have pleased and busied my selfe at idle houres" (page 11). This orientation apparently satisfied Burton for thirty years of revisions, though it may be that had he lived or had the strength to make further changes he would have had trouble keeping the section on love within his focus.

Is there any evidence as to where—many years before 1621 or even 1615—Burton began his desultory work? Almost immediately, certain sections can be eliminated like those on herb cures, the problems of nuns, and the nature of the passions. These and sections like them are medical or psychological in orientation and totally devoid of the kind of interest one would expect to find in the writings of a young humanist eager to make his mark on the world. It would seem much more likely that human folly was the first thing to attract his attention, or the possibility of planning the ideal state, or human behavior in adversity, or the benefits of travel, since these were the subjects that Renaissance humanists were writing about. There seems to be no way around the view that Burton's early training was humanistic and theological: we have the evidence of his library, his early studies, the curriculum at Oxford, and his own embarrassment over the study of medicine. It is not unlikely, therefore, that the original layer or *ur-text* of the *Anatomy* is made up of essentially humanistic essays—essays on the need for tranquility of mind, essays on anger, leisure, and the happy life such as Seneca too wrote; essays on benefices, studies, sloth, and friendship like those of Erasmus; essays on literary criticism like Jonson's; essays on subjects Selden liked to talk about—government, law, marriage, poetry, religion, and witchcraft.

To be more specific, it might be suggested that the series of "to see" passages in the Preface, where Burton describes various kinds of human folly, his comments on the corruption of lawyers, his analysis of English character and English resources, and the Utopia all may go back to an early stage. Still other passages from the First Partition might by such evidence be held early: the Pauline discussion of human misery, the digression of spirits (with its extensive treatment of folklore about witches), the bitter comments on the bad influence of parents on their children, and the observations about bad air and about the joys of sports and games. Each of these topics seems to have been the stock-in-trade of every Renaissance humanist-moralist, and none is organically a part of the problem of melancholia. Out of problems that Bacon also treated—imagination, discontent, covetousness, self-love, love of learning, scoffs and calumnies, poverty— Burton created perfect little essays of his own. The great digression, "Air Rectified," leaves almost entirely the theme of melancholy to concentrate on a subject of interest to the humanists and physicians who had founded Greek medicine and to the Roman architect Vitruvius; topics like exercise and games, travel and sports, music and interior design have only the most tenuous connection with melancholy; still other topics, like servitude and poverty, were more traditionally the province of the Stoic than of the psychiatrist.

One of the principal repositories for what is evidently an early layer of material are the many digressions which Burton managed to incorporate within his book. The idea of the "digression" is very old, and the ramifications of this phenomenon in literature are numerous. At least as old as Quintilian is the idea that a prime function of the digression was to make a work pleasant and delightful, "to add beauty to the speech," to achieve a great effect, and to delight the audience.[22] Laurence Sterne speaks of the digression as "the sunshine . . . the life, the soul of reading," and he notes enthusiastically that

all the dexterity is in the good cookery and management of them, so as to be not only for the advantage of the reader, but also of the author, whose distress, in this matter, is truely pitiable: For, if he begins a digression,—from that moment, I observe, his whole work stands stock-still;—and if he goes on with his main work,— then there is an end of his digression.[23]

Sterne boasted, "I fly off from what I am about, as far, and as often as any writer in Great Britain," and indeed, no author, not even Swift or Byron, has handled the irrelevant relevancy with greater effectiveness. What Sterne had discovered was, however, something more than a legitimate technique for enriching the texture of his writing. He had come to see the digression as an essentially quixotic device, recognizing the irony of putting a passage into a book not despite its irrelevancy but precisely because it fit so badly. By this technique Sterne was able to hint at the relativity of all values —perhaps even at a form of nihilism.

Now it is perfectly possible to see the Burtonian digression in this light, especially since the outline is there so prominently. It ought to be the function of an outline to force every bit of material to conform—to trim off all the edges before the literary suitcase is closed. One might conclude from the presence of both outline and digressions that Burton suffered from an almost comic inability to manage the most fundamental problems involved in writing a book: an unwillingness to decide once and for all what was significant and what had to be eliminated. Sterne's sympathy for Burton may suggest that there is indeed in the anatomist of melancholy a cynicism or an ambiguity about values that would make him such a quixotic author. But there is another side to Burton—his willingness to forego bitterness in order to speak seriously about situations that grieved him or about causes he sought to promote. At the very worst we must regard the Burtonian digression as a free ride on a hobby horse, as a chance to comment at length on favorite topics—the greed of patrons, the rascality of lawyers, the joys of books and boating. When these digressions are most rich, warm, and human they make the kind of affirmation of life that ought never to be allowed in a book on melancholy. They represent, I think, an early layer of material, too fascinating to be discarded, too irrelevant, even after a hundred visions and revisions, to gain a place in the structural fabric of the finished book.

But if the digressions and similar equally rich passages suggest that Burton's early interest lay in the liberal arts, it is evident that Burton moved steadily into other fields. Bergen Evans has suggested that Burton's primary interest was in mental health and (quite plausibly) that he saw the impossibility of eliminating melancholy until its social and cultural determinants were eliminated too. Evans contends that Burton's humanistic and social concerns were intrinsically a part of his interest in medical problems; I can accept this in only a limited fashion, for it has been my contention here that the idea of a book on mental health was a very late development. A move from the humanities to the study of society would, however, have been an easy and natural one, the interconnections between the two areas being very old. What happened to Burton may have been what happens to

many people who "go into literature" because they are
enamored of the subjective element but soon move out into
something more objective and in many ways more significant.
The celebrated image of the philosopher-king, which suggests
the need for a close link between the wisdom of the humanist
and the expertness of the public official, as well as the anal-
ogy between the state and the human body were apparently
old when Plato developed them. Many Renaissance moralists
assumed a correspondence between the spirit of man and the
body politic—Sebonde, Castiglione, Elyot, and Hobbes; and
Shakespeare makes the same point through the mouths of
Lear, Menenius Agrippa (*Coriolanus*), and Ulysses. It is,
therefore, as a kind of philosopher-king that Burton scorns
the utopias of the poets as too poetic and faces the practical
problems of the world outside his library. The most obvious
motivation of Burton's interest in social reform were the
problems that arose during the latter half of the reign of
James I and about which Burton continued to hear, as edition after edition of his book passed through the press. William Mueller, who has examined intensively Burton's interest
in social problems, points out that in the third decade of the
17th century English foreign trade collapsed, that unem-
ployment and depopulation (due to the enclosure movement)
were rising, and that economic confusion resulting from crop
failure, a surplus of gold, and constriction of manufacturing
were rife. In the years just before Burton wrote, a series of
popular uprisings occurred and the relation of wages to prices
fell off disastrously. In 1621, the year of the publication of
the *Anatomy,* some thirty statutes were enacted, all to no
avail, against the export of wool.[24] These facts suggest an
economic crisis of some magnitude and may place Burton's

emergence as a social critic in the second decade of the 17th century, in the dozen years before the *Anatomy* appeared.

As for the development of Burton's interest in medicine, I can find no evidence, except that which implies (as I have suggested and will further indicate) that it came late. Most of the medical books which might have influenced him very profoundly appeared about the turn of the century (too early to aid in dating), and it seems unlikely that one book like Adams' *Diseases of the Soule* (1616) could have produced such a change in Burton's point of view.

But change there was—a fact that is nowhere more clearly evident than in the Preface of Democritus Junior. Here is revealed vividly both the warfare and the cooperation at the heart of the *Anatomy* between the humanist and the physician-psychiatrist, as well as the long unresolved quest for power of utterance. It has been a common response of those confronted with the contradictions between the preface and the main body of the *Anatomy* to suggest that Burton, anticipating the practice of modern writers, composed his preface after he had finished the body of his book and had arrayed the material as it now stands into three partitions.[25] Such a view, however, is complicated by the fact that the preface is clearly not of one piece, but rather that it falls into several sections—a core (the long and fairly coherent essay on the nature of man), the Utopia within this core, and several incidental pages of introduction and conclusion fore and aft. The heart of the preface (pages 14–69 in the first edition) is a bitter examination of human experience. It is set off by the comment on page 13 about "the ensuing Preface" and it is ended by Burton's observation that while at one time he had certain reasons for writing a moral attack upon man, he is now done with describing melancholy metaphorically and will now deal medically with the actual humor. He also feels that his attack on man was too harsh and insulting. The brief section which follows this confession, like that which makes up the first pages of the preface, is biographical rather than philosophical and deals with such questions as motivation for writing and the preparation of the book for the press. In the pages at the very beginning and at the end of the preface —which I would guess were written just before the book was turned over to the printer—Burton devotes a great deal of time to himself: to his lack of talent, his long confinement in the university, his personal unhappiness, and his pose as a spectator. He is acutely self-conscious and acutely aware of his readers. Petty annoyances are aired (against selfish patrons and compulsive scribblers), and the personal pique which is revealed stands in vivid contrast with the massive rage of the middle section, a rage growing out of Burton's sense of the fundamental wrongness of the world. The prose of the first and last sections is curt almost to the point of incoherence, whereas the style of the middle section is calm and objective—if only to conceal the profound anger being expressed. But what is most significant of all is the absence in the middle section of any reference to the medical writers who eventually came to influence Burton so strongly.[26]

In this early section, the influence of the Abderite philosopher, Democritus, is strong: he seems to have symbolized for Burton the moral and humanistic tradition in which Burton was trained. Where he dominates, neither Bright nor Laurentius get in any licks at all. What we have here, then, is an old essay, written in Burton's "humanistic period" and later embedded in passages written just before the book was published. Having performed dissections and written about melancholy, Democritus was retained as an even more useful mask. Had Burton composed the entire preface when he completed his book, he could scarcely have avoided references to the medical aspects of his problem (physical causes being, as he sees it, the root of melancholy), and he would certainly have stressed much less strongly the moral aspect. While it is true that there are passing references in the original essay to such physicians as Montaltus and Jason Pratensis, these references are for moral and ethical, rather than medical purposes. Burton may have known Bright and Laurentius and other medical writers when he wrote his original essay on human folly but they had not yet come to dominate his thinking.

Through some such process as this Burton seems to have passed as he prepared himself for what eventually became a book on melancholy: the composition of desultory essays on topics of broadly humanistic interest, a developing concern over social and economic problems, and then a resort to "such Physitians our Libraries would afford" (page 6). And all the while there was the struggle toward some comprehensive and provocative position from which he could make a useful contribution to human well-being. It may be, of course, that behind his choice of melancholy as a subject there lay nothing but his own perverse statement that he wrote about melancholy in order to avoid it; he was evidently a man of Saturnine temperament himself. Whatever the causes (recognized and unrecognized) that were the basis for Burton's choice, it is clear that when the book was outlined and the preface readied for publication the point of view had been set once and for all. A treatise on divinity, which Burton feels may compensate for his secular interests, will have to be a book by itself. And even the expansion of the section on love—an expansion so massive that the development of another orientation is implied—cannot disturb the pattern, pull as it will in another direction.

How adequate was the problem of melancholy as a focus for the lifework of a late Renaissance humanist? This might be called a bad question, for it could be noted that here was a very distinctive point of view, highly productive of suggestive ambiguities, the source of much of Burton's quaint charm, a provocative way of looking at "the gallantry and misery of the world." But when the same question is put with an eye to the problem of Burton's potentialities, their release and their frustration, it becomes evident that here was a focus with serious drawbacks. It involved Burton with a great deal of material in which he was not really interested. It seriously handicapped his treatment of vital issues such as the ideal state, the nature of love, and the problem of leisure, for while melancholy could justify the introduction of such topics it could hardly support a full-dress treatment of them. It linked him to a fundamentally deterministic explanation of human behavior (though it must be admitted that for Burton "melancholy" covered a wide range of disturbances from minor temperamental problems to insanity). In this connection, it is worth noting that Pavlov, among other modern psychologists, approved of the theory of the temperaments. But other less deterministic and more dynamic theories of behavior were available: the voluntarism of Calvin, the stress of Hobbes and Descartes on the passions.[27] Erasmus had already spoken scornfully of the stone man whose fluids were in order but who was devoid of passions and emotions. Timothy Bright, a clergyman, was severely frustrated in his attempt to deal with human behavior in terms of humoral theory, and Robert Boyle, in 1661, was to undercut the theory of the cosmic elements, which underlay humoral psychology. Without appearing to demand of Burton that he possess the insights of a modern psychoanalyst, we may affirm that he was, in this area at least, something of a member of the old guard. As a world view, melancholy forced Burton into an essentially subjective attitude in what appears to have been an increasingly outward-looking age, and into a negative and critical attitude in an age that was essentially optimistic and dynamic. The great issues of Burton's day were the investigation and use of the natural world, the problem of adjusting individual liberty to state and church controls, and the nature of the ideal human community. The contributions which Burton made in these areas were made not so much because of but in spite of the focus he chose. For the quixotic quality which so delighted Romantic critics, Burton paid a fearful price: he never reached firm conclusions about the role of the scholar or the intellectual in society; he never adequately reconciled his own views with the views of most of mankind.

This confusion over a world view was quite naturally reflected in Burton's problems with his lifework. The Renaissance attitude toward vocation is never entirely clear, and it becomes quite muddy in the 17th Century with the decline of the humanistic tradition. There are, on the one hand, many records of men who were content to serve the time for what it would bring; Dryden may have been such a person; and Montaigne, in his essay on husbanding the will, presents the case for noninvolvement. We have, on the other hand, the evidence presented so eloquently by Professor Harbison in *The Christian Scholar in the Age of the Reformation* that some humanists approached their studies with a spirit of the deepest consecration. Thus, it is an open question whether or not the experience of finding a vocation held for 17th-Century man the same psychological implications that it holds today. While Montaigne can speak with some distress about the man who loses his inner being in some great lifework, within the Christian tradition there is no idea more hallowed than that of laboring at one's calling. This concern is reflected in the priestly dedication of the young Milton to poetry. It is to be seen in Browne's anxiety over reconciling his vocation as a physician to his Christian faith. It is to be seen in the sense of dedication which developed in Donne after he entered the ministry. Such persistent interest would seem to justify the examination attempted in this paper of Burton's struggle, through his scholarship and through a variety of academic disciplines, to bring the world into focus for himself. Burton's sense of frustration and meaninglessness was no doubt lightened by moments of joy and enthusiasm, but ultimately it brought him to double disaster—an intellectual orientation which was as frustrating as it was challenging, and suicide—by a tradition that goes back unchallenged to his own day. All the blossoming interest in new fields of knowledge, all the darkening of hopes, all the despair about the survival of wisdom in a lost world—all these responses of the modern humanist Burton felt too. His was the trying experience of more than one sensitive scholar of the Renaissance who grappled with mammoth problems, failed to make the necessary reconciliations, and lived out an uncommitted career with an unsettled mind.

Sir Thomas Browne: scientific data and mystical experience

3

Late in life and as a lonely Irish exile, Jeremy Taylor wrote a letter to John Evelyn in which he suggested touchingly how some men feed on books and ideas as eagerly as most men feed on more normal comestibles:

> But, Sir, I pray say to me something concerning the state of learning; how is any art or science likely to improve? what good books are lately public? what learned men, abroad or at home, begin anew to fill the mouth of fame, in the places of the dead Salmasius, Vossius, Mocelin, Simond, Rigaltius, Descartes, Galileo, Peirisk, Petavius, & the excellent persons of yesterday? [1]

A necrology that is virtually the obituary of the Renaissance! The nourishment that Taylor sought so pathetically was, in one form or another, the lifeblood of countless of his contemporaries. Ideas about every conceivable subject constitute one of the principal worlds which 17th century man had to cope with; here I describe the attempt of Sir Thomas Browne to reduce them to something with personal significance.

About the content and variety of 17th century thought there have been many books in recent years, but too often, it seems to me, the stress has been placed on what might awkwardly be called the "intellectual burden" of the ideas rather than on what they involved for those who held them —what commitments they demanded, for example, or what powers they released. Ideas, like words, operate at a denotative level: they convey instructions for specific actions, they are weapons in controversy (with more or less exact meanings), and they are useful in constructing philosophical systems. In all of these cases they are quite properly subjected to intellectual analysis: it is necessary to examine the source of each part of the idea, the connections between the parts, and the relationship of the idea to one's sense of reality.

But ideas are also connotative, poetic, suggestive; they induce and mirror states of mind with which a man faces his experience of the world. Vaughan's notion of paradise was not part of an intellectual framework, any more than Marvell's love of green or Herrick's delight in May Day. Taylor no doubt mulled at length over the idea of personal piety, just as Herbert must have found comfort time and again in the Anglican ideal or Milton considered the problem of liberty. But even though these men were writers of the greatest skill, they never (in all probability) succeeded in expressing that something buzzing at the back of the brain, which welled out of the whole breadth of their experience.

And indeed, through words, no man ever has. Certain movements of the human brain are ineffable: they will not yield
up their secrets to the clumsy intellectual tools which we
possess. But this fact need not doom all thinking and talking.
The function of an idea may not be to contribute to an
analysis but to be the vehicle of a certain impatience with old
ways, a wish to experience new modes of being, or a sense of
repose or disturbance. To assume that all men have organized
the world of ideas in the same way or for the same purpose
is to lay oneself open to grave errors in estimating one kind
of human experience.

   This distinction is probably an obvious one, yet it has often
been overlooked. And no one has suffered more than Sir
Thomas Browne at the hands of admirers uncertain about the
many things that can be done with ideas—especially speculative ideas. It was widely held throughout the Renaissance
that advanced thinking was a threat to the ordered human
community. Taylor, softening this conservative view slightly,
declared that "high speculations are as barren as the tops of
cedars; but the fundamentals of Christianity are fruitful as
the valleys or the creeping vine." [2] Milton is careful to have
Raphael warn Adam sternly to avoid subtle questions, but
he also takes note of Selden's comment that "all opinions,
yea errors, known, read, and collated, are of main service and
assistance toward the speedy attainment of what is truest." [3]
For all its dangers—real or assumed—the speculative habit
was an inseparable part of the revival of learning. If on the
one hand speculation was seen as a futile activity that seemed
to imply rebellion against the established order, it also became a popular game, which involved finding answers to
questions as obscure as they were hoary: why there were no

horses in America, what name Achilles assumed when he was
hidden in the harem, why there are owls in Africa and not in
Crete, where Springtime goes, whether Homer was blind,
Penelope a whore, Helen innocent. University students debated these issues, poets turned them into elaborate compliments for their mistresses, and mature humanists continued
to hope that from them some useful knowledge might ultimately be derived. Meric Casaubon, son of the great French
humanist, wrote a notorious essay on the walking stick
($\beta\alpha\kappa\tau\eta\rho\iota\alpha$) in ancient times, thereby abusing knowledge as it
was not to be abused again until Cardinal Newman's brother
translated "Hiawatha" into Arabic. But there were also significant results: the speculations of earnest thinkers about
witchcraft, occultism, prophesying, ancient pagan philosophy, and the status of the clergy led ultimately to proposals
for religious toleration, brave stands on the subject of witch
burning, and the composition of important poems. Francis
Bacon, an expert here, suggests in many passages from his
books what a wide experience the typical 17th century man
had with ideas. He used them to construct great philosophical
systems or theatres (which all too often he then assumed
represented absolute truth); he became expert in the application of detailed information to limited problems; he
learned how to apply a broad range of general insights to the
management of complex affairs; he used his knowledge to
impress others, to amuse himself, and to carry on his business.
It is against such a background that I propose the thesis of
this chapter: that Browne employed his speculative or discursive intellect not to create philosophical systems or to
make philosophical analyses, and not even (primarily) to
solve scientific or theological problems, but to induce in him-

self a state of ecstasy through which an ultimately liberating,
unifying, and noetic experience might come.

I. Browne's religious orientation

A study of religious psychology reveals basic similarities of
technique among those who in different parts of the world
and at different times of history have sought a mystical experience. Thus it is that we would be very much surprised to
learn that Browne had an acquaintance with Oriental techniques for inducing ecstasy, but we are not at all surprised
that he, like some of his contemporaries, had come to be
aware of certain forms of psychological and spiritual power
which are decidedly non-Western and exotic. This awareness
has been attributed to a certain affinity of creative people
"for what in most of us is unconscious or preconscious" and
to the dissatisfaction that some feel that in our culture
certain "precious potentialities were left to die at birth." [4]
Whatever it is that so profoundly attracts us to Oriental
religious thought, the fact is that expressions of roughly
parallel attitudes and states of mind are not as rare in Western literature as might at first be imagined. Goethe's *Faust*,
Cervantes' *Don Quixote*, the American Transcendentalists
have all been seen to reflect a more or less Oriental feeling
for other modes of being. Nor is this spirit lacking in the
17th century.[5] Take an anecdote like Burton's story of the
man who came to a tree bearing a rope, intent on hanging
himself. Finding a pot of gold at the root, he ran away with
his treasure, leaving the rope for the owner of the gold who,
when he missed his money, hanged himself. Or again, in

Burton's own words, consider the tale of "that *Egyptian* in *Plutarch* when a curious fellow would needs know what he had in his basket. . . . It was therefore covered, because he should not know what was in it." Both of these *jeux d'esprit* bear comparison with the little Zen stories which have become so popular in recent years:

> A Monk told Joshu: "I have just entered the monastery. Please teach me."
> Joshu asked: "Have you eaten your rice porridge?"
> The monk replied: "I have eaten."
> Joshu said: "Then you had better wash your bowl." [6]

Different as content and context may be, the effect of each story (whether from Burton or the Mu-mon-kan) is surprisingly similar. Each is at first hearing flat, empty, and unsatisfying. But as the quixotic, irrational truth penetrates the consciousness, a wry, wan smile begins to flicker on the lips. Disturbance follows frustration, puzzlement follows disturbance, and then comes exotic pleasure and insight. A human situation, an occasion, a passing moment has been illuminated in a most unexpected way.

One interested in drawing other kinds of parallels might compare Marvell's description of his relationship to Nature, in "The Garden,"

> What wondrous life is this I lead!
> Ripe apples drop about my head;
> The luscious clusters of the vine
> Upon my mouth do crush their wine;
> The nectarine and curious peach
> Into my hands themselves do reach;
> Stumbling on melons, as I pass,
> Ensnared with flowers, I fall on grass.

> Meanwhile the mind from pleasure less
> Withdraws into its happiness;
> The mind, that ocean where each kind
> Does straight its own resemblance find;
> Yet it creates, transcending these,
> Far other worlds and other seas,
> Annihilating all that's made
> To a green thought in a green shade—

to the observation of one student of Buddhism that "Zen leads to a unified awareness" in which knower and known become one, and that the Zen gardener has no intention of forcing his wishes upon natural forms but carefully follows the "intentionless intention" of the forms themselves, clipping, weeding, and planting in the spirit of the garden itself." [7] Suzuki says, "There is nothing in the Zen master's *kyogai* [environment] which differentiates itself as something wondrous or extraordinary. It consists, as in all other cases, in scenting the fragrance of the laurel in bloom and in listening to a bird singing on a spring day to its heart's content. What, however, makes a difference in the case of a Zen master is that he sees the flowers as they really are and not in a dreamy sort of way in which the flowers are not really flowers and rivers not really flowing rivers. Pure subjectivity, instead of vaporizing realities . . . consolidates everything with which it comes in touch." [8] It is precisely such a relationship with Nature that the lines from Marvell describe.

Finally, there is the matter of suggesting rather than stating fully what one means; this is an issue where literary form plays an important part, and even here it is possible to find parallels between what Oriental poets and 17th century poets have done. Consider Herrick's fragile lines,

> Her pretty feet
> Like snails did creep
> A little out, and then,
> As if they started at bo-peep,
> Did soon draw in again.

with a poem in the Haiku style:

> On a withered branch
> a crow has settled—
> autumn nightfall.[9]

These passages seem to suggest that even in an age as rationalistic, as sophisticated, as word conscious as the 17th century, some writers were making a place for the quixotic, were concerning themselves with the implicit and the symbolic, were finding significance in action that was spontaneous, uncalculated, and completely natural. The important point about Browne, therefore, is not so much that he treated religion experientially (which he did), or that he was a mystic (which is a generalization so broad as to be meaningless), but that he lived in an age when even sober scientists and clergymen were taking note of experiences that lay well beyond the bounds of the scientific and the rational.[10] This may help to explain why Browne, too, used the most unlikely kinds of data—mathematical, geometrical, and physiological—to induce the mystical experience. This point needs to be stressed, for too many who have written about Browne have concentrated on an analysis of his ideas and have missed the important thing: what he used these ideas for.

Thus Miss Wiley declares that "Browne was caught up in an exciting search for truth," and she sees him reacting to "the faintest glimmerings of truth, climbing to the dizziest heights and risking all for the integrity of his own spiritual experience." E. S. Merton suggests that Browne was embarked on a lifelong quest, driven by a pure "Hellenic love for truth." Professor Dunn has described the *Religio Medici* as a serious and courageous attempt to express views that were unpopular during the Puritan regime, and as "certainly something more than a subjective study of the paradoxes of metaphysical beliefs." [11] Admitting that Browne is not to be systematized and that he has no significant place in the line of English thought, Dunn nevertheless deals seriously and at length with Browne's treatment of the problems of faith and reason, with his view of the natural world, and with his psychology. It is certainly right to talk seriously about Browne—if one can view his paradoxes seriously too; it is right to see him seeking for truth—if one is willing to admit that "truth" may not be precisely the right word for the kind of nonverbal experience which Browne was seeking; and I think it must be recognized that Browne's mysticism may have been essentially a psychological matter, as mathematical as it was religious, no more theological than biological. Modern critics have been far too anxious to use Browne's work as a vehicle for the projection of their own deeply felt needs for charity, for a spirit of toleration, and for religious faith in the face of modern science to see Browne's ideas for what they really are.

D. K. Ziegler, to my way of thinking, comes closer than anyone else to stating the truth about Browne as a thinker. Ziegler's little book, *In Divided and Distinguished Worlds* (the title comes from Basil Willey's discussion of Browne and ultimately from the *Religio Medici*), was published in

1943 but has been unjustly neglected since that time. Frank Huntley, whose recent book on Browne carries the attempt to integrate Browne's various interests to extreme lengths, cites it and then goes on about his business without meeting its incisive arguments. There are reasons for this neglect. In the first place, Ziegler argues that Browne made a complete divorce between science and religion, and that he thought clearly as a scientist but confused his understanding of religious affairs by a love for mystery. Whatever links Browne made between the two worlds he made emotionally, not intellectually. Such a view can hardly be expected to be popular among the modern irenecists who, in their zeal to heal breaches between science and faith, often overlook the width of the chasm. (This chasm, of course, has a curious way of widening and narrowing as one advances from stage to stage in his understanding.) What is more, Ziegler tends to make Browne into a 17th century positivist, interested in religions for the aesthetic stimulation which they provided but caring little for any ultimate truth to which they might point. Browne, Ziegler thinks, found the truths of science (grounded as they were in matter) more real than the truths of religion, and observes that in his splendid rhetoric, foolish or illogical statements about both spiritual and scientific problems are often hidden. Though he may overstate his case, Ziegler is the only modern student of Browne who has asked what to my way of thinking are the right questions. His approach moves Browne very definitely out of his Western orientation into a more exotic tradition, where religion means something quite different from what it normally means to us. F. C. S. Northrop has described Hinduism as based not on a series of dogmas about God but on indeterminate

aesthetic responses, on a "tranquil sensuality," on a cath-
olicity of spirit, on a refusal to believe that heaven is closed
to people who are not in the group, and on an interest in con-
versing with people rather than in converting them. I find
much of this applicable to Browne as well.[12]

II. Psychology of religion

This is not to make Browne a Hindu, nor is it to deny that a
great deal of his prose work exists at the normal levels of
prose statement. Very often, for example, Browne concerns
himself with the solid facts which are necessarily the basis of
any sensible person's construction of the world:

I am, I confess, naturally inclined to that which misguided zeal
terms superstition: my common conversation I do acknowledge
austere, my behavior full of rigour, sometimes not without moros-
ity.[13]
Of these four members of religion we hold a slender proportion
(II, 358).
Unspeakable mysteries in the Scriptures are often delivered in a
vulgar and illustrative way (II, 391).

He speaks in a rational, analytic fashion:

Where there is a manifest disproportion between the powers and
forces of two several agents, upon a maxim of reason we may
promise the victory to the superior (II, 344).

He makes aesthetic and moral judgments:

I hold there is a general beauty in the works of God, and therefore
no deformity in any kind of species or creature whatsoever (II,
342).

Persecution is a bad and indirect way to plant religion (II, 359). This trivial and vulgar way of coition . . . the foolishest act a wise man commits in all his life (II, 438).

There are "pious ejaculations":

Yet is God the true and infallible cause of all (II, 346).
The sufficiency of Christian immortality frustrates all earthly glory, and the quality of either state after death, makes a folly of posthumous memory (III, 46).

But observations like these, even when supplemented by Browne's obscure learning and his splendid rhetoric, would not have preserved his name to this day. He fascinates us because he convinces us, as we read, that he is on the trail of something much more important.

His own statements about his quest—his declaration of love for an "O Altitudo"—have not been taken seriously enough. For a supposedly learned man, he makes the most amazing statements: "I love to lose myself in a mystery" (II, 332). "Where I cannot satisfy my reason, I love to humour my fancy" (II, 333). Having perused all religious doctrines, he can "discover nothing that may startle a discreet belief" (II, 349). Strange ideas, he says, have been bred "amongst the weeds and tares of my own brain" (II, 377). He is willing to give chief credit to "dreams, thoughtful whisperings, mercurisms, airy nuncios or sympathetical insinuations" (III, 65). He knows about "Christian annihilation, ecstasies, exolution, liquefaction, transformation, the kiss of the spouse, gustation of God, and ingression into the divine shadow" (III, 48), and he declares that no one can think of eternity "without an ecstasy" (II, 334).

We get an even clearer picture of the direction in which Browne was headed when, in addition to this confession of a desire to be "confounded," he spells out a very positive dislike of academic issues. He feels, for instance, that there is little need to think about heresies, since there is so much that is nonheretical for an honest reason to consider (II, 332). He declares it foolish to expose one's life for some intellectual trifle (II, 360). He simply cannot grow angry with someone who disagrees with him (II, 326). And in the interpretation of important theological terms like "anima" or "lux" he prefers an imaginative or poetic interpretation to an abstract definition: to describe the soul as the "messenger of man" ("angelus hominis") he thinks preferable to description of the soul as "entelechy" (complete actuality). He recognizes that there are intellectual impossibilities: Homer wisely did not worry about the riddle of the fishermen, Aristotle was able to live with the problem of the flux of Euripus, and let the pedants explain the flood, the absence of horses in America, the great age of Methuselah, and the death of Judas— Browne will accept them all as problems and rest in faith. Bacon had called questions like these "vermiculate" or "worm-eaten" and had declared them examples of the "disease of intellect." Doubtless they merited the scorn of one interested in useful, scientific truth. But behind Browne's lack of interest in these particular issues I see something else—recognition of the fact that not all matters of intellectual speculation had the power to wrench the mind out of its normal discursive operations into contact with radically different points of view, absolutely new modes of thought. And so I return again to my thesis, that for Browne, ideas were chiefly important when they could serve as avenues to

ecstasy or enlightenment, to states of dizzy reeling, to a sense
of the numinous, to contact with some primal force. To at-
tain similar states, some mystics have used drugs, the Greeks
used the music of the flute, other seekers have practiced
various forms of *ascesis*.

A fuller explanation of what I believe Browne was up to
demands some digression into the psychology of religion and
into areas where the practice of many religions seems to take
a common path. The ultimate concern of religion has been
variously defined, but a common goal would seem to be the
achievement of what has been called "the new being," an
entry into radically different relations with the Ultimate,
with the world, with one's fellows. The Christian tradition of
the saint is a testimony to the reality of this relationship, as
is the tradition among the Sufi mystics of the Arab world and
the Chinese Buddhists of the "fool of God" or the "mad
master." From the Orient there comes the peculiar instrument of conversion or enlightenment known in Japan as the
Koan and in China as *hua t'ou*. These terms refer to a statement or to the answer to a question given by a Zen master
which is intentionally obscure, baffling, and direct—as direct
as the contact which Martin Buber describes between the I
and Thou. The *hua t'ou* or "flame against flame" technique
is a statement, purposefully ludicrous or baffling, which is
designed to destroy the verbalizations by which a student of
Zen might try to *think* his way toward enlightenment. Luk
calls it "a pointed concentration to cut down all thought," [14]
and it is used in much the same way that Roman Catholic
mystics use the "Name of Jesus." When it has focused attention on genuine reality and rid the mind of the tendency to
verbalize, it is allowed to drop away. (There is a Zen story

about a drowning monk who was given two paddle blows—
one to remind him to think about saving his life, one to rid
him of even that thought.) Both the *Koan* and the *hua t'ou*
are instrumentalities through which, it is hoped, the torpor
in which most human beings live will be pierced, so that the
energy and the insights which lie deep in the subconscious
can be released. This power is freed, it is felt, only when the
logical, calculating mind, the mind that operates through
syllogisms and dualisms and traditional identifications, is
destroyed or quieted. Martin Buber tells the story of Rabbi
Israel Baal Shem Tov, who warned that other rabbis hinder
the redemptive work of God by talking too much, and Suzuki
makes the same point when he says that the function of Zen
training is to stop the "hankering, monkey-like mind from
doing mischief." [15] A comparative study of techniques of
mysticism or enlightenment in all the major religions would
doubtless reveal much agreement on methods, though there
are, even in Zen, differences of stress: thus Luk suggests that
the *hua t'ou* should be observed with the same steadiness that
a broken tile plunges deep into a well. Hui-neng, the Chinese
founder of Zen, condemned, on the other hand, keeping the
eye on anything that can dominate thought and stressed a
kind of seeing that brings seer and object together.

Sometimes *koans* are terribly flat and "devoid of flavor":

Who is the Buddha?
Three chin of flax.

(I have been told that the Chinese word for "No" ("Mu"),
which is very rich in connotative values, has been used with
Western students as an object of meditation, but without

success.) Sometimes *koans* are maddeningly baffling and seemingly irrelevant:

> What is the meaning of the first Patriarch's visit to China? The cypress tree in the front courtyard.

Sometimes, when an old hand needs rousing, the challenge can be brutal:

> Take a step forward from the top of a hundred-foot pole.

Paradox is frequently employed, as well as observations that are intentionally irrational. Sometimes the teacher "creeps up" on truth, without either asserting or denying anything. Fundamental, however, would be the refusal to grasp at stratagems, the attempt to block out all active thought, and submission to a veritable death of the mind. As frustrations begin to accumulate, the student becomes highly wrought and experiences vomiting or sickness in other forms. At this point he may burn his books, leave his master, try to find some sly method of drawing his bow, or abandon the course completely: he cannot wait for the slow, natural operation of spiritual and psychological forces within himself. But this is just the moment when enlightenment or *satori* may occur —through a tiny tap, the blow of a stick, the master's shouting "Ho" or "Kwats" (or remaining perfectly silent), the sound of a bamboo broom striking a rock, drinking tea, leaving (or not leaving) when the time has come, being hurled into a stream, or being pierced to the heart with a sword. Enlightenment is achieved directly, not by slow stages.

What this state brings is described in various ways. Verbal

descriptions have been declared inadequate, yet it is often said, too, that the experience is in no way mysterious or tranquilizing. Some have found a "turning of the mental hinge to the wider and deeper world," while others insist that now this world is seen as it really is. Luk suggests that with the experience comes escape from the world of doing, and from the claims of thought, and from the long strain of self-cultivation. Watts argues that with this state all compulsions are eliminated, the "blocked up" feeling is destroyed, and a measure of simplicity—the ability to go ahead spontaneously—is achieved. Roger Godel describes the "liberative experience" in these words:

The freed-alive knows the indestructibility of true life, that life of which he experiences the nontemporal essence. The human state resolves itself for him into the Unconditioned. His beneficent radiation—of love and knowledge—exerts itself with absolute disinterestedness upon the beings who approach him. He stimulates in them, silently or by speech and the lesson of his own life, the search for the true.[16]

The idea of nothingness occurs frequently in descriptions of the condition which is achieved, though it is persistently denied that this state (which is by some called "Nirvana") refers to annihilation; rather, it is seen as a state of unobstructed consciousness, where self, will, and arrogance are all absorbed into a profound sense of altruism. Through this experience, the normal categories in which men live—space, time, cause, effect—are transcended; all entanglements of desires and passions are extinguished; and now is felt "the Presence par excellence of the Unique, of the Only Real, Transcendent and Unknown until He wills to reveal Himself." [17] The richness and peace that come with letting go of the self eliminate all desire for further enlightenment. All available evidence suggests that the pattern which so many people have attempted to describe is by no means confined to the Zen sects, or to the East, or to any period of history. Insofar as this enlightenment is a universal experience (universal, at least, among those who possess the patience and wisdom to achieve it), we are justified in asking to what extent it was known by Browne, as well as how he tried to achieve it with the instrument of speculative thought.

III. Browne's method in religion

Browne's method, from all that can be gathered, was essentially verbal. He did, of course, have a museum of curios which might have provided "objective correlatives" for his ideas: he notes that he found Regiomontanus's tiny mechanical fly more suggestive than his mechanical elephant, he cannot forget the opal found in the urn at Walsingham, and he is always touched by the sight of the crucifix. By and large, however, he will be found turning over some paradox: "the world was before the creation, and at an end before it had a beginning. And thus was I dead before I was alive; though my grave be England, my dying place was Paradise; and Eve miscarried of me, before she conceived of Cain" (II, 413). Or again, "Could the devil work my belief to imagine I could never die, I would not outlive that very thought" (II, 381). He likes to employ a technique which the Chinese call "going beyond opposites," finding truth outside normal affirmations and negations: "I hold that God

can do all things: how he should work contradictions, I do
not understand, yet dare not, therefore, deny" (II, 362). Is
the distinction between left and right inherent in Nature?
he wonders. Then again, he can be found trying to apprehend
some great abstraction in physical terms: conceive the distinct number three, he urges, "not divided nor separated by
the intellect, but actually comprehended in its unity, and that
is a perfect trinity" (II, 336). But a more normal avenue
to contact with some reality beyond that of normal experience is to be seen in Browne's many attempts to establish
some radically different angle, to see things from some fundamentally fresh point of view. What will it be like, for those
who never heard of Adam, to be condemned for his sin? Can
that "secret gloom or bottom of our days" (II, 387) be re-
covered and made a telling part of the present scene? Persistently Browne argues that the processes of Nature are
broader, more comprehensive, more all-pervasive than modern man has generally recognized. The secret workings of
Fortune are, therefore, a common topic—the cryptic and
involved form of God's providence, "that serpentine and
crooked line" (II, 343). Browne is aware that "unexpected
accidents slip in, and unthought-of occurrences intervene"
(II, 344), and he affirms " 'tis not a ridiculous devotion to
say a prayer before a game at tables; for, even in sortileges
and matters of greatest uncertainty, there is a settled and
preordered course of effects" (II, 345). Because our eyes are
too dim to discover "the mystery of her [Fortune's] effects,
we foolishly paint her blind, and hoodwink the providence of
the Almighty" (II, 345).

The Chinese mind, it might be noted (since we have already moved in this direction), is apparently much more

willing to recognize the operations of Chance or Fortune than the Western. I have been told by a highly sophisticated professor of linguistics of the old school that there can be no question about the influence of the stars on human life. The typical Chinese thinker is not particularly impressed by the causal processes leading up to an event, for he recognizes each moment as a "chance hit," the product of forces which he feels he can never identify completely. Less attention is given, therefore, to how events evolve than to the interplay of the various parts of a situation as they intertwine with each other. An attempt to work out the end results of various chance combinations was made in the ancient Chinese text, *I Ching,* or *Book of Changes,* in which a series of trigrams [☰☰ ☷☷ ☵☵] etc. are presented in some sixty-four combinations, each representing some situation faced in life. By study of the diagrams and the interpretative matter, responses might be planned and precautions observed. Browne, however, is not interested—as far as I can see—in predicting the future; his concern is with the effect produced upon the human mind when one suddenly realizes that his life is the product of "infinite rubs, doublings, and wrenches" which may look like chance but may be the hand of God. It is not surprising that he found the labyrinthine turnings of the story of Joseph "able to convert a stoick" (II, 343). Browne's positivism appears in his concern with the psychological effect rather than with the actuality of a belief.

An even more striking example of the use of an idea to produce a sense of numinous transcendence is offered in *The Garden of Cyrus,* called by some a bad book, but nevertheless the interesting result of an attempt to look at the world

not monistically or dualistically, or as infinitely diverse, but
in terms of fives, of decussations, and of rhomboids. Five, it
has been noted by a student of Chinese painting, is the maximum number of objects that the eye can grasp at one glance;
more than five trees become a grove; five is a compositional
maximum.[18] And Whitehead claims to have had clarity of insight and "intimate friendship with" the first five numbers,
but he notes that the Indian mathematician Ramanujan had
each of the first hundred integers as a personal friend.[19] It may
be, then, that Browne was attracted by the way the number
five maintained its wholeness while tottering all the while on
the brink of sheer multitude, or it may be that as a follower
of Pythagoras he was touched by the mystical significance of
the number. Whatever the basis of Browne's interest, he begins his book with an account of the quincunxial arrangement
of gardens, tracing next the figure in "sundry artificial con-
trivances and manual operations" (II, 506), finding that
architecture is founded on fives, that gems are cut into fives,
that bandages are decussations, and battle wedges rhomboids. The works of Nature he surveys next—stars, stones,
plants (which have one set of leaves growing out of the stem
at right angles to the next set), the motion of butterfly
wings, the movement of a circle—all demonstrate the
quincunx. Trees, he observes, are planted in the quincunx
pattern to provide maximum light and root space, and even
their cylindrical trunks suggest the "long round" of the
parallelogram. This discussion of trees and shade leads
Browne to an obscure passage on the arrangement of colors,
specifically the blues and greens which are so easy on the
eyes—the colors of mediocrity. Noting that white is the
dominant color of plants below ground, Browne observes

how this white spreads out to green at ground level, and how this green shades over into the blue of the sky. He appears to see in this arrangement, as in the way darkness and light dominate the "seminal state of things," a hint of the quincunx. There follows a rhapsody in which Browne seems to see fives everywhere—it is the conjugal number, the number of radical letters in the Pentateuch; five thousand persons were fed with five loaves; water and wine are mixed in proportions of three to five; Antonius thought the soul a rhombus. Finally, Browne offers his reader an invitation to meditate on *"quaternios . . .* to erect generalities, disclose unobserved properties . . . [in] the whole volume of nature" (II, 562). What one can abstract from quadrates is hard to say, but from the quincunx Browne has drawn the generalization that the fabric of the world can ultimately be reduced to alternates coming in endless succession. This may be depressing, but there is something dizzying about it, too.

Some other of Browne's favorite topics for speculation should be noted, though admittedly without his powers of rhetoric such a listing will be bare. One such topic would be the relationship between archetypal form and material reality. Browne was obviously a Platonist, with a firm belief in patterns and archetypes, and no existentialist. He pictures that moment on the last day when "our separated dust, after so many pilgrimages and transformations into the parts of minerals, plants, animals, elements, shall, at the voice of God, return into their primitive shapes, and join again to make up their primary and predestinate forms" (II, 395). He notes the probability that the form of a leaf is not destroyed when the leaf is burnt (II, 396), and he finds that "In the seed of a plant, to the eyes of God, and to the understanding of man though in an invisible way, there exists the perfect leaves, flowers, and fruit thereof; for things that are *in posse* to the sense are actually existent to the understanding" (II, 401). When Browne put archetypal reality over against material fact, he was apparently fascinated and dazzled by the clash of categories and the consequent ambiguity of "reality." His dilemma recalls the comment of Laotse on the tension between the forms of things and their origins or that principle of modern physics which declares that the speed of a particle and its location cannot both be determined at the same time.

The rich connotations of *circles* appear to have touched Browne very deeply. On the one hand there is the idea of emptiness: he is fascinated by the blank spaces on the "thin-filled maps" of the Saxons (III, 14). Then again there is a touching reference to dying (as Browne did) on the day of one's birth: Browne is deeply moved that "the tail of the snake should return into its mouth precisely at that time, and they should wind up upon the day of their nativity" (III, 69). Browne's reference to the snake biting its own tail appears frequently in Egyptian art, as well as in many primitive and later European cultures. Technically the symbol is known as the "uroboric circle," and its presence in Browne suggests a number of things. It points to his interest in one of the most intellectually chaotic systems ever devised by the human mind—Hermeticism. Like Vaughan, Browne toyed most of his life with the dazzling circles and lights of this ancient faith, in love with it, says Schultz, because it preserved so well a sense of the essential mystery of life.[20] The uroboric circle suggests, too, the process of reproduction which so fascinated Browne—that "great work whose wonders are second only unto those of the Creation," which made the universe buzz and tingle with life. On a psychological plane, the snake symbol, which appears to be related to other enclosing symbols such as caves, wombs, and coffins, brings to mind the many circumscribed areas from which life emerges and to which it returns. Erich Neumann has written that this symbol depicts the unformed, chaotic condition of the human personality before it achieves adulthood or full consciousness—the state of primal unconsciousness in which the sleepy, unborn ego exists before birth.[21] It was to just such a state, where the huge and the overpowering were dominant, where the waking, conscious mind was pleasurably engulfed, that Browne intended speculation should lead him.

Browne appears also to have found thinking about time, eternity, and number highly suggestive. Time, only five days older than man, he finds comprehensible enough; the real intellectual thrill lay in the idea of eternity: "to retire so far back as to apprehend a beginning . . . puts my reason to St. Paul's sanctuary: my philosophy dares not say the angels can do it" (II, 334). Speculation about numbers fired him too, and in *Vulgar Errors* he devotes considerable space to their meaning—one (unity), three (trinity), four (the letters in God's name), six (the days of creation), and ten (combining even, odd, long, plain, quadrate and cubical numbers) (I, 12). The idea of threeness (Browne's interest in it has already been noted) has about it a dazzlingly mystical sheen, a power of opening up new layers of consciousness which the other numbers, no matter how patiently they are contemplated, do not possess. Browne, as might be expected, was deeply interested in the work of Pythagoras, the Greek mathematician, and Whitehead helps us to see the significance of this interest. Pythagoras was the first to realize the importance of number in representing the idea of Nature, the first to ask important questions about the status of entities like numbers, the first to see how numbers are both exempt from the flux of time and yet deeply involved in the world of reality.[22] Without the sophistication of the modern mathematician or the profundity of the Greek, Browne nevertheless recognized in speculation about numbers a ready vehicle out of the world of physical reality into realms of pure being.

From an interest in what numbers could suggest, Browne moved easily over into "the book of creatures," "the stenography of nature," the "signature of all things." His interest in the Hermetic doctrine that "this visible world is but a picture of the invisible" (II, 336) has already been noted. Browne was especially moved by the minutiae of the natural world, pointing out that admiration of the large externals of God's work is "gross rusticity" and that it is only by "deliberate research into his creatures" (II, 338), that the significant, microscopic wonders are to be found. Browne's interest in theories of generation and his sense of the hidden kernel which imparts motion to life tends to underscore the point he makes about observing "all Africa and her prodigies in us" (II, 340), and seeing in the minute details of the body a vast, geometrically increasing source of possibilities for contemplation. E. S. Merton has written informatively and at length on Browne's important place in the development of 17th century theories about generation. Here is one of the few areas where Browne spoke as an authority. It was also an area to which he could respond imaginatively: meditation on the fecundity of the natural world very quickly suppresses the waking, conscious mind and effectively destroys the pretensions of the rational faculty.

But for Browne the most suggestive of all ideas was Death, for here more than anywhere else were combined the most touching and mysterious parts of life—beginning and end, the chaos of our forebeings and the ecstasy of being ever, dark and light, the tiny womb and the boundlessness of Heaven. Death was for Browne what the idea of Greece was for Keats—"a most dizzy pain . . . the rude/Wasting of old Time . . . a billowy main—/A sun—a shadow of a magnitude." As a philosophically minded physician, Browne could do little more than face death manfully. As a poet, however, he could contemplate the exquisite irony of "the thousand doors that lead to death" or reach out eagerly for it as for the one moment when a man fully realizes his Being —the moment when a man is both nothing and "within one instant of a spirit." An unpublished comment which Dunn found in one of the manuscripts of the *Religio Medici* is very revealing: "It is a symptom of melancholy to be afraid of death, yet sometimes to desire it; this latter I have often discovered in myself, and think no man ever desired life, as I have sometimes death." [23] Just what was the kernel of death's meaning for Browne remains uncertain. Browne says that belief in the resurrection is essential to any firm religious faith—indeed, to any will to live. But it has been the argument of this chapter that Browne was perhaps interested chiefly in the *idea* of resurrection, an idea that can thrill even those who have little faith in the actuality. And from the evidence assembled here, from Browne's interest in sleeping and dying, it would seem that the idea of absorption into boundless light or dark, into the cloud of unknowing, into that without beginning or end was what touched him most deeply. Some ideas Browne used for scientific purposes; others were stairs to ecstasy.

There have been varying estimates of Browne's success in penetrating into some new state of being, some deeper level of consciousness. Professor Dunn seems to feel that the issue is closed: "Our physician is revealing himself as a full-fledged mystic. . . . It would appear then that Browne thus early is committed to something very like mysticism. . . . Browne is carried into a mystic region where the body and the material universe itself is simply a subjective phase of spiritual life." [24] Ziegler, on the other hand, will go no further than to grant that Browne was in love with the idea of mysticism; he never achieved this state himself. My own feeling is that Browne knew enough of mystical enlightenment to desire further experience, but that the tools he was using were too easily misapplied, especially where a master who might have directed his steps was not available; and where there was missing an understanding of the fearful cost in frustration, concentration, and obedience to Nature's way that he would have to pay for what he was seeking.

In his most sustained effort to use ideas as a path to enlightenment, *The Garden of Cyrus,* all that he has done is to assemble the data; he has "asked his master the question," which is no mean feat in itself. But then, instead of the all-essential directed silence, he has thrown the whole thing up and written that beautiful passage about sleep closing the five ports of knowledge. Our searcher has thus broken a cardinal rule of Zen and indeed of all forms of spiritual questing: Keep Awake! Though the injunction applies primarily to spiritual waking, it is obvious that such a state de-

mands physical waking too.[25] But this movement is symp-
tomatic of what happens time and again in Browne as some
developing insight is smothered in bravura rhetoric:

'Tis the debt of our reason we owe unto God, and the homage we
pay for not being beasts (II, 338).
In brief, all things are artificial; for nature is the art of God (II,
342).
I have so fixed my contemplations on heaven, that I have about
forgot the idea of hell; and am afraid rather to lose the joys of
the one than endure the misery of the other (II, 402).

It might be said that Browne's meditations lacked, ultimately, that animation which comes through grace or through
the Holy Spirit or that for Browne contemplation was an
activity of his being, not being itself.[26] Or it might be said,
following Teilhard de Chardin, that Browne never pushed
his spiritual and psychological growth to that "critical
point" where emergence onto new levels of reality could
have occurred.[27] Browne's world offered ideas ripe for mystical exploitation and some comprehension of certain unusual
levels of reality at which a man might live. But Browne
seems to have lacked that knowledge of religious psychology
(a knowledge he might have come to intuitively) essential
for the experiment he was undertaking. He succumbed, a
budding amphibian, to the great temptations which his age
offered—the temptations to reduce ineffable insights to words
and to couch these words in the grand style. A unique experiment in the ordering of scientific and scholarly data did not
succeed.

Pilgrimage to Paradise: center of Vaughan's religious world

4

In times of profound cultural change, men often face uncertainty about what elements of experience can be built into the pattern of life as sources of creative power, what elements will prove to be frustrating blind alleys. John Stuart Mill's case illustrates the dilemma of the man trapped between early rationalistic training and a deep-seated emotionalism. Voltaire, by nature an optimist, was forced toward pessimism by the evils he saw in his world. Within similarly mutually exclusive pressures worked Henry Vaughan, and this chapter will attempt to describe those elements of experience which he found meaningful and to assess the significance of the decisions he made. In his recent book, *Henry Vaughan and the*

Tradition, Ross Garner pictures Vaughan as moving between a number of very specific poles: between belief in God's immanence and his transcendence, between the experience of a religious faith and a theological faith, between pessimism and optimism, between mystical longing and mystical fulfillment.[1] The simplicity of my own feeling about Vaughan's experience—that his important choice was for an inner-directed, evangelical religion rather than an institutional, theological faith—not only reflects my conviction about the actual source of Vaughan's poetic power but is also a protest against the overly complex analyses that we are getting today from some readers of Vaughan. Criticism of this beloved poet-physician normally and quite understandably begins in a strong personal response. But it seems to end all too often in ceaseless, semantically oriented, self-sustaining debates about mysticism and Hermeticism which shed consistently less light on Vaughan and suggest that he was a much more complicated person than his work would lead us to believe.

If one is seeking full knowledge of the life of a particular Welshman who happened also to be a poet, the problem of his service in the Civil War, the nature of the lawsuits he faced, the date when he began his medical practice, and his relationship to his brother Thomas are all issues that would need to be considered. Certainly no slighting of Hutchinson's biography, a labor of love, is intended by such a remark. Fundamentally, however, these problems lie on the periphery of the poet's experience and personality. At a deeper and more significant level lie the Anglican tradition within which Vaughan lived, the doctrines of the hermetic philosophers in which he dabbled, the untrammeled experience of the Welsh countryside which he enjoyed, and his sense of the moral decay of his society. Then again there are a few things which seem to have mattered very much indeed to the poet—the death of his brother William in 1648, which Vaughan interpreted as a solemn and sacrificial warning to himself; possibly a long sickness before he completed *Silex Scintillans* (1650); certainly his reading of George Herbert; and his conception of life as a pilgrimage to Paradise, an image that haunted and comforted him all his life. When we step into the mystery-haunted Welsh world of Vaughan, we leave behind many of the things that matter much to most men; in place of the strident sounds of the busy, outer world, we hear once again waterfalls in forest depths; the cock wakes us at dawn with its cheery note; mists blanket the tops of low-lying hills; and we find ourselves embarked on that journey of the heart which spiritual pilgrims in every age have made.

Recent students have assessed and reassessed the meaning for Vaughan of all these things, at the same time neglecting other matters that seem to me to be of more than incidental importance. In particular, I detect in Vaughan a persistent strain of middle-class, low-church, evangelical piety, an element which clearly has something to do with the kind of Anglican Vaughan was, with his understanding of the human condition, and with the patterns of his imagery. This, then, is the issue to which this chapter addresses itself—how the outer shell of the high-church tradition to which Vaughan belonged gave way to something that owed more to the tradition of Pietism, William Langland, and Dante than to the school of Herbert and Andrewes. It is hard to use terms like "middle-class" and "evangelical" without seeming to suggest sociological or economic factors like belief in private property or stress on industry and thrift, or without seeming to imply that Vaughan would have made a good Salvation Army major. And certainly no suggestion that the Anglican communion has neglected to preach the Gospel is intended. There is no good single word, however, which embraces all that I have in mind: the tendency to link religion with such virtues as thrift and temperance; stress on the acceptance of a certain body of theological doctrines which give primacy to the Bible both as a source of doctrine and as a devotional book; adoption of the traditional pattern of religious life as comprising a wasted youth, a definite experience of conversion, and a holy later life; and a concern with the apocalyptic and the personal aspects of religion. In Vaughan, the religious point of view which embraces elements like these—to which the poet adhered with his whole heart—is set against a highly sophisticated, definitely intellectual, communal faith to which the poet apparently gave his outward devotion.

I. Anglican and Evangelical strains

Vaughan's relationship to the Anglican communion would have to be regarded as an important element in his experience if only because of the present widespread (but not universal) agreement that Vaughan was at heart a religious poet who had found himself by reading George Herbert, a devout Anglican. But even those modern readers who insist on the sincerely religious nature of his work will probably agree with Eliot that for Vaughan Anglicanism was really of less than primary importance. A great deal of what Vaughan has to say about the church is essentially negative—attacks, for instance, upon its enemies. Much of Vaughan's wrath is, quite naturally, directed against the Puritans, for their ugly treatment of their father (Charles) and their mother (Anglicanism). Vaughan was outraged by the insolence of the mob at the death of Strafford; he hated the zeal and spiritual pretensions of the Puritans ("Who Saint themselves, they are no *Saints*"); [2] he was annoyed by the way they boasted of special insight; he was troubled by their pride (in "The Throne" he notes that on Judgment Day "the most/Stiff then must kneel"—p. 533). In "Ad Posteros" he complains about the *tempora dura* which the Puritans imposed upon Wales, referring to the commission appointed by the Propagation Act of 1649/50, which removed many of Vaughan's friends and neighbors from their posts and left spiritual desolation throughout the country. And in "The Proffer" he is apparently rejecting with scorn the offer of some government post under the commonwealth. Vaughan is proud of the burdens he has borne thus far and scorns those from whom the proposal has come as "poys'nous, subtile fowls!/The flyes of hell . . ." (p. 487).

There is, of course, more to Vaughan's Anglicanism than his dislike of the Puritans. A number of poems in *Silex Scintillans* celebrate the holy days of the church year, and Holy Communion is praised as a sweet and sacred feast. But as a sacramental poet, a poet concerned with presenting in a truly compelling fashion the real personal and communal benefits flowing from Christ's sacrifice, Vaughan is not at all effective. The degree to which he failed to respond to traditional religious symbolism is suggested in any number of stanzas, in which the extent of his failure is perhaps best gauged by the absence of anything that really sounds like the true Vaughan. The "Easter Hymn" begins with a kind of jingle:

> Death, and darkness get you packing,
> Nothing now to man is lacking,
> All your triumphs now are ended,
> And what *Adam* marr'd, is mended (p. 457).

Throughout "The Passion" Vaughan appears to be more interested in his stanzaic structure than in his meaning:

> O blessed Lamb!
> That took'st my sinne,
> That took'st my shame,
> How shall thy dust thy praises sing! (p. 431)

And there is nothing more (or less) than an absence of personal conviction wrong with lines like these from "The Holy Communion":

> And now by these sure, sacred ties,
>   After thy blood
>   (Our sov'rain good,)
>   Had clear'd our eies,
>   And given us sight;
> Thou dost unto thy self betroth
>   Our souls, and bodies both
>   In everlasting light (p. 458).

Stanzas like these suggest the condition of large sections of most Protestant hymnals today, where doctrine is presented in language and imagery that are no longer very relevant or meaningful and may indeed be positively offensive. When Vaughan writes this way he lends support to the conclusion of some modern scholars that in the 17th century there was a definite decline in the power of religious symbols to catch up and center the attention of believers upon a meaningful creed relevant to the needs of an entire community. They reveal a poet not acting consistently with value schemes that he had chosen, a poet writing for a time on what Gordon Allport has called "the periphery of his being." [3]

In the Middle Ages the Eucharist had provided for poets a body of truly analogical symbols in which a genuine, organic correspondence between symbol and object was felt by all worshipers. But, as Professor Malcolm Ross has demonstrated, the 17th Century witnessed a pronounced decline in the power of religious symbols to sustain the vital synthesis which Hooker had worked out between all phases of human existence—the personal, the national, and the divine.[4] In part, this decline can be traced to the Reformation, which made the Bible generally available, and with it a potential source of material for banal and sentimental versifying by people lacking power to penetrate to the heart of the message. But the Bible was only a contributing cause; Roman Catholics had their bleeding hearts and it has always been a common human tendency to dilute or soften the hard lines of strict and meaningful belief. In any case, medieval symbolism lost its power to synthesize and provide meaning for life, and only through the artificiality of the Baroque and the spirit of Pietism was strong feeling—strong, but fundamentally divorced from life—preserved. Professor Ross finds in Milton's Samson a brief recapturing of the old multileveled symbol, but in general he feels that phrases like "the body" and "the blood" had ceased to mean very much. Signs of the loss of a sense of unity, accompanied by growing subjectivism, can be detected, thinks Professor Ross, even in such a high-church poet as Herbert; in Vaughan the trend becomes quite pronounced. Not the high-church text, "The word was made flesh and dwelt among us," but quite another injunction, the evangelical "Marvel not, ye must be born again," lay at the center of Vaughan's religious experience. If Anglicanism was one of the weaker forces operating on Vaughan, we must eventually come to an assessment of his success within another religious tradition.

Another factor in Vaughan's experience which has not received adequate treatment is his sense of social corruption and personal sinfulness. We know that Robert Burton found his society foolish, corrupt, depraved, and slothful, and what I have been able to discover about the condition of Wales in the 17th century does not suggest a society that was fundamentally different from that of England itself. The order and the religious faith which many people today associate with Wales came with the rise of Methodism, long after Vaughan's death. David Williams, in his study of Wales, suggests that in his country the Reformation meant very little, having been accepted largely because there was no strength to fight it.[5] John Rhys and David Jones present a dismal picture of Welsh life at the beginning of the 17th century: "There were an indifferent upper class, a clergy wretchedly paid, of low moral and spiritual type, and a people ignorant to the first degree." [6] In facts such as these lies a more than adequate basis for whatever sense of human depravity Vaughan may have felt. Now the 20th century has grown accustomed to judging its theologians by the intensity of their diagnosis of evil, and much the same thing might be said of the tragic poets, whose task it is (in part) to show that the evil which

men see all around them is part of the same evil which they
sense within themselves. Similar, too, is the task of the metaphysical poets, which is to order the world as it confronts
them by transmuting the objective into the subjective, social
evil into personal evil, apparent evil into ultimate good. The
constant preoccupation of the great poets with these inter-
changes makes me wonder why Ross Garner has been so
troubled about discovering the origins of Vaughan's pessimism and reconciling it to his optimism. The view of man
as broken, twisted, overwhelmed by sin is as essential to the
Christian view of man as is the Christian hope that somehow
man's sinful nature can be transformed.

It is perhaps one measure of Vaughan's less than complete
success as a religious poet that he never—or rarely—manages to see social corruption and sin in the theological sense
as parts of the same strand of evil. He makes good poetry
out of human folly, and he makes excellent poetry out of the
Christian's sense of sin, but neither issue is allowed to illumi-
nate the other. He misses something here that other Anglican
poets saw. The extended poem, *"Isaac's* Marriage," does not
get much beyond sarcastic references to contemporary social
practices: Vaughan expresses surprise that Isaac should have
prayed before marriage; oaths and compliments, he complains,
are much the more normal rule on such occasions. The chastity
of Isaac's bride and the plainness of her dress also appear to
surprise Vaughan: he is much more accustomed to *"rowles
and Curles"* (p. 409). In the poem "Content" he makes
other remarks about dress ("Why then these curl'd, puff'd
points,/Or a laced story?"), and he finds another manifestation of such an obsession with the insignificant in the "queint
folies, sugred sin" (p. 446) which comprised the "Idle

Verse" he wrote as a young man. An extended examination of the human plight appears in "The Tempest," where the way man is "parcell'd out" is described and the suggestion is advanced that many moral lessons are to be learned from Nature. But man prefers darkness:

> Yet hugs he stil his durt; The *stuffe* he wears
> And painted trimming takes down both his eies,
> Heaven hath less beauty than the dust he spies,
> And money better musick than the *Spheres* (p. 461).

The most famous attack upon social vice in Vaughan is probably that vivid set of "characters" which make up the central section of Vaughan's greatest visionary poem, "The World." In this somberly magnificent portrait gallery, Vaughan describes many whose errors and blindness have made it impossible for them to rise up through the great ring of pure and endless light. The doting lover is presented, the miser on his dust heap, and the "darksome States-man, hung with weights and woe." Those who live in the "vast shadow" are victims of destructive passions and humors—the folly of loving what is unworthy, pleasure hunting, spiritual blindness, choler, melancholy, secret ambitions, deceit, indifference, fear, greed, and gluttony. Vaughan's concern with social evil was genuine, but he was never able to give the vice he recognized any metaphysical significance. As a social satirist Vaughan demonstrates nothing of Donne's ability to endow his material with multiple meanings; rather, he moves toward the rigid single-leveled expression characteristic of Francis Quarles in his *Emblemes* (1635). Emblem books, it is generally conceded, were designed for middle-class tastes and expressed a middle-class morality in

acceptable intellectual terms. Vaughan, Garner notes, "seems
to have thought" in emblems, and lines which Quarles wrote
for one of the engravings in his book are certainly suggestive
of Vaughan:

> One hugs his gold; another lets it fly:
> He knowing not for whom; nor tother why.
> One spends his days in plots, his night in play;
> Another sleeps and slugs both night and day (I, 8).

Even when Vaughan turns to the problem of personal sin,
he continues to think along the same line—sin is excess, folly,
the result of some errant bodily fluid (choler, phlegm), the
harm wrought by something seen with the eyes. Sleeping at
midday is a characteristic image of the human condition, or
groping blindly for something, or stagnating like a corrupt
puddle, or being hurled restlessly back and forth like a loom:

> At length I feel my head to ake,
> My fingers Itch, and burn to take
> Some new Imployment, I begin
> To swel and fome and fret within (p. 473).

Life is described as an "*Inne*/And Rode of sin" (p. 442), the
poet himself is "a Ward, and still in bonds" (p. 397), and
man is a heap of crumbled dust or an idiot called hither and
thither by many voices, sleepily hugging the dust he loves so
well, unable to distinguish the specious from the genuine.
The human body is described as a broken box, as an inn
lashed by winter rain; the stars which once offered clear
direction have closed up shop; the rooms of the mansion
have grown dusty and desolate with the landlord's absence or

become places where we "careles state/With folded hands"
(p. 416). On winter walks through Brecknockshire, Vaughan
has felt the stench of black leaves and weeds drenched with
cold showers, and he has had his "perspective glass" clogged
with mists. With great candor he confesses, in "The Hidden
Treasure," that were it not for fear of "the dreadful brink"
he could have made splendid use of all that the world offers:

> Man's favorite sins, those tainting appetites
> Which nature breeds, and some fine clay invites,
> With all their soft, kinde arts and easie strains
> Which strongly operate, though without pains,
> Did not a greater beauty rule mine eyes,
> None would more dote on, nor so soon entice (p. 520).

We miss in Vaughan's treatment of evil the medieval splendor of Spenser, the awesome grandeur of Milton's sense of
universal chaos, the terrible pathos of Dante's Inferno, that
sense of the living voice of the sinner raised in rebellion
which Donne so vividly achieves. This is the poetic side of
Vaughan's deficiency. Theologically, the weakness lies in
Vaughan's failure to realize the power of sin to pervert the
will and to blind the understanding and to break man's link
with God. Sin, as the passage just quoted suggests, is all too
frequently seen as appetite, and only rarely as the willful
destruction of spiritual ties. Occasionally one finds lines in
Vaughan which capture the genuine horror of evil:

> The Turtle then in Palm-trees mourns,
>   While Owls and Satyrs howl;
> The pleasant Land to brimstone turns
>   And all her streams grow foul (p. 497).

But these lines, while undeniably effective as poetry, would hardly mean much to a theologian. Typically, I suppose, evangelical Protestantism has never comprehended the full breadth and depth of even this world's Hell; for all its talk about wormlike man, it is essentially an optimistic faith, buoyed up by the good news it has heard. It remained for Dante, a very unusual Catholic, to fall before it *"come corpo morto cade,"* and for Kierkegaard, a very extraordinary Protestant, to describe the full terror of human alienation from God. Vaughan stood too far away from his material for either the tragic or the satiric vision. Spiritual lethargy, an inability to feel in one's heart the glow of God's presence, not being "saved"—these are the important things in the evangelical tradition to which Vaughan was heir.

This viewpoint is perfectly consistent with the whole of Vaughan's grasp of theological truth—his preoccupation with the Fall (seen both historically and individually), which has been noted by E. C. Pettet, his belief in the doctrine of predestination and its distinction between the elect and the nonelect, and his sorrow over "the inevitable decay of religious feeling." [7] Pettet avoids calling this set of beliefs Calvinism, although that is just about what they are, and what Vaughan has done is what a good many other near-Calvinists have done—toned down or smoothed out the rougher edges and sharper angles of their creed. And if for Vaughan, as for every evangelical Christian, the sense of lethargy, of loss of contact with God, of falling away from a state of Grace is the prime indicator of man's sinful state, so in Vaughan, especially since he is a poet, a sense of freshness, of seeing once again, of Spring, of blossoming, of communion—these are the great and positive religious experiences for saved men. W. C. Doughty's discovery (reported by Ross Garner) of "My soul, there is a country" in the "Love and Communion" section of the Methodist Hymnal is the kind of thing that could almost have been predicted beforehand. This is exactly where Vaughan belongs, what with his deep-seated love of the Old Testament (that part of the Bible so dear to the more radical side of Protestantism), his own profound experience of conversion, his persistent concern with the evangelical theme of pilgrimage. I for one among many absorbed the same tradition in the little Sunday School room with its green, threadbare rug, its sandbox desert, and its soapcake Palestinian houses in my grandfather's church. Vaughan loves nothing so much as the Psalms, stories of the journeys of Abraham, the trials of King David, Jacob's dream, Elijah's ravens, Moses on Mount Sinai, Noah's rainbow, and "those calme, golden Evenings" when the patriarchs watched their flocks (p. 406). This is a faith which saw Nature through the eyes of Solomon and the author of the Book of Job, a faith bedazzled by apocalyptic visions nourished on Ezekiel. It is a faith grounded in a set of awesome theological abstractions tempered by homely concerns and a never-failing interest in the common ventures of life. It is a faith with a peculiar language of its own—being "hid above with Christ/in God" (p. 490), bearing the cross, being blessed by "Sun-shine after raine" (p. 413), and receiving from the Bible "a sudden and most searching ray" (p. 541).

Vaughan, of course, is not to be explained away as the poet of a simple religious faith. His journey and his hope are parts of a far more complex and sensitive reconstruction of the outer world than most people who share, or have shared, his point of view are capable of. Lethargy is a perfectly respectable sin, being numbered among the deadly seven, and Vaughan's experience of it and his escape were matters of genuine anguish. The still point which Vaughan ultimately found for his turning world was a very complicated set of memories of childhood, grief at the human situation, and hope for eternity. And if Vaughan did not make the grand metaphysical synthesis, he does convey modestly that sense of ties and linkages which characterizes metaphysical poetry. There is, for example, the sense of paradox—the old Christian paradox, for instance, that being God's prisoner is perfect freedom (p. 472); there is, in Vaughan's feeling for Holy Communion, a grasp of the opposites out of which every profound human experience is constructed:

> . . . Healings, and Cuts,
> Darkness, and day-light, life, and death
> Are but mere leaves turn'd by thy breath (p. 457).

There are the striking comparisons which are so characteristic of metaphysical poetry: Sundays are pulleys for men, or lamps, or "transplanted Paradise" (p. 447), or God's "parle" with dust, or honeycombs of rest or, stupendously, "the milky way Chalkt out with Suns" (p. 448). There is, too, that sense of metamorphosis which so interests the poet concerned with the nature of reality: man sets out to find (or "track") God and finds that God is the tracker; Christ is both food and Shepherd for his sheep; and in the eyes of his dead brother it is the living Henry who has now become dust. Most important, though, is the sense of order and unity which Vaughan feels so strongly, in part at least because of his interest in Hermeticism: "Sure, there's a tye of Bodyes," he affirms (p. 429), and when morning comes

> . . . all is hurl'd
> In sacred *Hymnes,* and *Order,* The great *Chime*
> And *Symphony* of nature (p. 424).

When Vaughan was at his best, he transcended any kind of religious orientation with which he might be saddled, presenting fully that passionate sense of existential experience transmuted into deep inner meaning, which is the mark of every true poet.

II. *Pilgrimage to Paradise*

I have been noting the presence of a profound and pronounced evangelical strain in Vaughan, basing my argument perhaps somewhat tenuously on a number of isolated facts, most of them centering, ultimately, on Vaughan's persistent view of life as a pilgrimage or a journey. The connection between the image and the evangelical tradition should be established before any attempt to examine Vaughan's use of the metaphor is attempted. A suggestive examination of the pilgrimage image has been made by W. H. Auden in a little essay ultimately directed at the elucidation of Franz Kafka, but in the process embracing many forms which this motif takes. In the fairy quest, for instance, some object with magical powers is sought by a hero who is successful where others before him have failed. In the quest for the Holy Grail, a knight is sorely tempted to settle for more immediate, less spiritual powers; the object of the dream quest (Dante) is some spiritual good; the peculiar quality of the Faustian quest for necessity is a complete lack of religious authority: the goal is certainty, and the method is to explore every possibility. In the Kafka quest, the problem is to discover just what one is searching for.[8] Now the Vaughanian pilgrimage, insofar as it seeks the reality behind appearances, resembles the Dantean quest, but it resembles even more closely the pilgrim's progress, where every man's journey is unique, where every man is solely responsible for his own safety, and where a good deal of the success depends upon the vigor with which the journey is pursued. Vaughan's poetry similarly breathes the voluntaristic, individualistic air of evangelical Protestantism.

William Haller establishes cogently the connection between the pilgrimage motif and the religious mode which is the subject of his book, *The Rise of Puritanism:*

The Puritan imagination saw the life of the spirit as pilgrimage and battle. The images of wayfaring and warfaring which fill the Old Testament had been exploited by that fighting itinerant, Paul, and by generations upon generations of subsequent evangelists. Reaching the pulpits of the seventeenth century by a hundred channels, they there underwent new and peculiarly vigorous development. The occupants of many of those pulpits would undoubtedly have tried to enforce their ideals by law if they had had the power. Lacking the power, they had to dwell upon the responsibility of the individual for enforcing them upon himself. They told him that his soul was a traveler through a strange country and a soldier in battle. He was a traveler who, fleeing destruction, must adhere through peril and hardship to the way that leads home. He was a soldier who, having been pressed to serve under the banners of the spirit, must enact faithfully his part in the unceasing war of the spiritual against the carnal man.[9]

The two most famous pilgrims in English literature—Spenser's Red Cross Knight and Bunyan's Christian—

walked through English sermons and devotional guides with many less well-known figures. Images of "spiritual" travelers appear frequently in Quarles' *Emblemes:* two young travelers groping through the darkness of this world, travelers in peril at sea, a young person threading her way through a labyrinth but cheered by the exhortation, "Pilgrime, trudge on" (IV, 2), and Christ and the soul ranging the fields to enjoy the season's delights. Thomas Taylor made the image basic to his little book, *The Pilgrims Profession* (1622), as did Arthur Dent, author of *The Plaine Man's Path-Way to Heaven* (1601), and Thomas Goodwin, who wrote *A Childe of Light Walking in Darkness* (1636). For Goodwin, who does less with the journey motif than one might wish, the problem of darkness is crucial, as it is for Vaughan. Darkness can mean distress of conscience, a lack of assurance of justification, inner and outer sorrow, stumbling, fearing, or being in doubt about one's next step. Vaughan's pilgrim suffers the same agonies. In his emphasis upon the work of Satan (the cause of the darkness), Goodwin differs radically from Vaughan and probably indicates the nature of his audience, but in his images of light and in such homely descriptions as that of God's grace being "chalkt out" in the Bible, the preacher constantly suggests the poet. In Dent's discussion of the human condition, we find again the subject matter of Vaughan: the corruption of the world is spelled out, the role of God's grace, the need for thrift, the wickedness of lying, drunkenness, and idling. These vices, along with their corresponding virtues, have been traditionally associated with the middle class, and with Calvinism and its offshoots. Louis Wright's observation, in *Middle Class Culture in Elizabethan England,* that in the early 17th century

"London citizens found moderate Calvinism best suited to their inclinations" [10] will not, perhaps, make a Calvinist out of Vaughan, but it may help to point out the links between him and a group toward which he felt both animosity and deep-seated sympathy.

From the viewpoint of earthbound man who sets out on his journey toward Paradise, perhaps the most fundamental problem is that he does not know exactly where or what his goal is. He must struggle to see what is lost in the distance, to hear what comes to him only very faintly. To remember what has been lost in time, to track things down, to travel ahead bravely when in despair, to be lost but always to keep one's will from bending—these are particularly difficult tasks for the kind of half-blind and sluggish person whom Vaughan has described. The tension of this experience was well presented by Francis Thompson, near the close of *The Hound of Heaven*:

> Ever and anon a trumpet sounds
> From the hid battlements of Eternity;
> Those shaken mists a space unsettle, then
> Round the half-glimpsèd turrets slowly wash again
>   But not ere him who summoneth
>   I first have seen. . . .

But Thompson's Gothic trappings have somehow slipped askew, and the modern reader is more likely to be deeply touched by Dante's images of the effort to pierce secrets and to comprehend what is only dimly perceived—images which capture with great effectiveness the questioning and questing mood of the pilgrim. Of seeing, Dante says,

'Twas now the time when the air was darkening, yet not so dark
but that what between his eyes and mine before was hidden, now
grew clear.[11]
From glasses transparent and polished, or from waters clear and
tranquil, not so deep that the bottom is darkened, came back the
notes of our faces, so faint that a pearl on a white brow cometh
not slowlier upon our pupils (p. 415).
Each looked at us, as in the evening men are wont to look at one
another under a new moon; and towards us sharpened their vision,
as an aged tailor does at the eye of his needle (p. 81).

And of hearing,

Just such impression gave me that which I heard, as we are wont
to receive when people are singing with an organ, and now the
words are clear, and now are not (p. 246).

And of mental activity,

Motionless we stood, and in suspense, like the shepherds who first
heard that hymn. . . . No ignorance, if my memory err not in
this, did ever with so great assault give me yearning for knowledge
(p. 309).

As we enter Dante's completely foreign world, these homely
comparisons become a source of enormous comfort; indeed,
such intersections of the trivial and the cosmic are one of the
sources of Dante's power. Vaughan's problem never involves
finding a lost self in quite the way Dante's did; his concerns
are the somewhat simpler ones of seeing behind masks and
shadows to the reality beneath, distinguishing the specious
from the genuine (the primrose is a frequent symbol of deceit), of piercing into the secret workings of God in Nature,
and, of course, of constantly pulling himself together and
moving ahead into the darkness of the unknown.

When Vaughan promises that "you might tread the Sun," he is asking the reader to envision a very special kind of walking—really a magnificent striding. Dante, too, was fond of picturing the many ways in which questing men walk:

We paced along the lonely plain, as one who returns to his lost road, and till he reach it, seems to go in vain (p. 198).
So we entered by the gap, one in front of the other, mounting the stairway, which by its straitness parts the climbers (p. 340).
We were alongside the ocean yet, like folk who ponder o'er their road, who in heart do go and in body stay (p. 202).

But Vaughan considers all the experiences of the traveler, not his pace alone. The poet describes the terrors of the path which leads through "a wildernes,/A Sea, or Sands and Serpents" (p. 468) and of the road "through darkness, dens, and mire" (p. 513). He condemns "foolish ranges" which no matter how much ground they cover can never lead to security, and he notes that some travelers are lured away by that "foolish fire," the *ignis fatuus*. He shares the perplexity of pilgrims lost at night, who weep as they measure the sky:

> Stars are of mighty use: The night
>   Is dark, and long;
> The Rode foul, and where one goes right,
>   Six may go wrong.
>   One twinkling ray
>   Shot o'r some cloud,
>   May clear much way
>   And guide a croud (p. 423).

Touchingly he describes the coming of dawn and he greets the sun as a fellow pilgrim:

> . . . all night have I
> Spent in a roving Extasie
> To find my Saviour (p. 405).

Sometimes, however, the desultory quality of "roving" is intensified: Vaughan speaks of racking his soul to find God and his soul's home; and he describes the way his "striving eye" "dazzles" at the thought of childhood (p. 520). But at best there come only glimpses of the goal—"that shady City of Palme trees" (p. 419), "that Cities shining spires/We travell to" (p. 423), or a Paradise seen in dreams.

Such stress on seeking and struggling gives definite intensity to Vaughan's experience; we feel constantly the pressure of a strong will being exerted. The sense of what can happen in a man who manages to rouse himself is paralleled in the Hermetic philosophy by the doctrine of the dynamic power of Nature to perceive, sense, and respond to God. A favorite figure of Vaughan's is that of "disemboweling" Nature, so that he may, if possible, discover where this power of fervent response to God lies:

> Herbs sleep unto the *East,* and some fowles thence
> Watch the Returns of light (p. 429).

Moreover,

> "Each *Bush*/And *Oak* doth know *I AM*" (p. 436).

The irony is further heightened as Vaughan observes of man,

> "th' herb he treads knows much, much more" (p. 469),

and as he remembers that according to Hermeticism, magnets are stones "which in the darkest nights point to their homes" (p. 477). Such is the origin of Vaughan's often expressed wish to be absorbed into the natural order, to become "some *Bird,* or *Star*" (p. 442), ready to be anything if he can experience the ecstasy of being ever. This, too, is why he is willing to be judged by Nature, content to be found inferior to

> The blades of grasse, thy Creatures feeding,
> The trees, their leafs; the flowres, their seeding;
> The Dust, of which I am a part,
> The Stones much softer than my heart,
> The drops of rain, the sighs of wind,
> The stars to which I am stark blind (p. 449).

Of the quiet but intense judgment of Nature against man, the laggard pilgrim, "Cock-Crowing" is the finest and perhaps most characteristic expression.

But when man does wake up, his longing is intense enough! Vaughan's scattered prayers, "Hadst thou/Made me a starre, a pearle, or a rain-bow" (413) . . . a stone, or tree (432) . . . grind this flint to dust! (462) present not only Nature's quiet condemnation of man but also the strength of desire with which Vaughan contemplated the state of salvation. Never, perhaps, does his yearning for some kind of consummation or settlement draw from him Donne's Michelangelesque cry,

> At the round earth's imagined corners blow
> Your trumpets, angels, and arise, arise
> From death, you numberless infinities
> Of souls, and to your scattered bodies go. . . .

Never, like Dante, does he cower before the red glow of the City of Dis or the terrible vengeance of Ugolino upon his tormentor, but as he contemplates, his peaceful rainbow becomes a blazing, vengeful comet, and with an inspired sense of sound values (the ominous long *i* of "fire") he weeps:

> Yet I know well, and so our sins require,
> Thou dost but Court cold rain, till *Rain* turns *Fire* (p. 510).

The poet achieves intensity through images of contrast (the single star interlining "night's gloomy page"); through images of concentration about a focal point (as he describes the earlier joys of the now lifeless timber); through images of vastness (among them the striking vision of eternity and the wonder expressed at the mighty progressions of the stars). Frequently Vaughan captures the feeling of some intense activity: the end of the world is proclaimed by "white winged Reapers" (p. 511), while the intimacy of the communion between God and man is suggested in words that bring to mind Francis Thompson's "Kingdom of God":

> Angels lay *Leiger* here; Each Bush, and Cel,
> Each Oke, and high-way knew them,
> Walk but the fields, or sit down at some *wel*,
> And he was sure to view them (p. 440).

Vaughan also puts to effective use the idea of confinement or compression as a means of suggesting the longing of his soul for clear vision and for communion. Only by the alchemic term "tincture" can the overwhelming sense of God, which is infused in the tiny cock, be described; the star's brilliance and vastness become for the poet symbols of its restless search for purity; the constellations are seen as spies of God; and the thick dampness of the cave is always pierced by a single ray:

> If a star were confin'd into a Tomb
>   Her captive flames must needs burn there;
> But when the hand that lockt her up, gives room,
>   She'l shine through all the sphaere (p. 484).

I suppose Vaughan had in mind here the tomb that held Christ—the tremendous force there confined, the vast light covered by close darkness, "life . . . locked in death, heaven in a shell."

But man, as Evelyn Underhill has pointed out, does not want to peep but to live, and Vaughan has lived indeed, conveying his experience of Paradise, of the "still, soft call," of the place "where I'd be" in splendid positive images. Vaughan's temperament, I would judge, pretty well excluded the kind of union with God which is the ultimate goal of the mystics, but beyond its Protestant, evangelical strain, there were depths far deeper than any religious dogma. One evidence of the archetypal quality of Vaughan's experience is his persistent concern with water, especially as it is seen in his poem, "The Waterfall," where "transparent, cool and watry wealth" (p. 537) issuing from the depths of the silent forest recalls the ideas of cleansing, of life, of insight into the ultimate meanings of things. Rivers and fountains, Miss Bodkin points out, have frequently been employed as symbols of the overflowing abundance of Paradise, and the rising and falling of water may suggest both the rising and falling of spiritual vitality and the undulations of the body, remembered from a time before birth.[12]

Still other evidence of the depth of paradisal element in Vaughan is provided by Mircea Eliade in his essay, "The Yearning for Paradise in Primitive Tradition." The "paradise myth," Professor Eliade notes, is found in some form all over the world, usually as the story either of an original proximity or of an actual contact between heaven and earth. All of the myths discussed by Eliade reveal the pattern, too, of a fall, and they picture prelapsarian man as enjoying "immortality, spontaneity, liberty, the ability to ascend to Heaven and 'easy access' to the gods, friendship with the animals and knowledge of their language." [13] Other significant aspects of what Eliade calls the "paradisal syndrome" (which he finds to be the heart of primitive mysticism) are the existence of the shaman or spiritual expert and the possibility of a state of ecstasy, in which the body is abandoned, space and time are left behind, and the mystical journey to heaven is made. Though I know nothing about the primitive roots of Hermeticism, I see certain parallels between it and the viewpoint which Eliade is describing: the shaman becomes the Hermetic adept; the talking animals become the intensely sentient world which the reader of Vaughan knows so well; the bodiless journey becomes the vision described in "The World"; and the fall becomes the great shadow within which the world is tossed. The final point which Eliade makes concerns the interest of Christian mysticism in the same paradisal theme: his conclusion that there exists "complete ideological continuity between the most elementary forms of mystical experience and Christianity" [14] neatly makes the connection about which I am concerned at this point.

A third indication of the depth of the paradisal chord in Vaughan is his persistent habit of thinking about Heaven in terms of being hidden, of enjoying intimacy with God, of finding the place of final security. Just as Ezekiel ate the scroll on which God's message was written, so Vaughan has made his longing for Paradise something peculiarly his own.

It is in secret that herbs are renewed and put on their youthful greenness, that ancient alchemic symbol of the wholeness of natural man. It is in secret that the seed grows. In secret God hides as he counts the tears of grief shed by man. On pages both concealed and protected by dust the record of his brother's quiet life is preserved. And after His baptism, Vaughan speculates, Christ surely sought some

> . . . happy secret fountain,
> Fair shade, or mountain

and, therefore, He loves to come still to "a narrow, homely room" (p. 516). Vaughan is touched by the intense privacy of the Mount of Olives: it becomes his bower of bliss, his favorite symbol of true but hidden beauty. Surely, though, "The Night" is Vaughan's greatest expression of this idea, and the last stanza the most touching statement in our language of this longing for mystical absorption:

> There is in God (some say)
> A deep, but dazling darkness; As men here
> Say it is late and dusky, because they
>   See not all clear;
> O for that night! where I in him
> Might live invisible and dim (p. 523).

Still further evidence of the seriousness with which Vaughan regarded the idea of Paradise is to be seen in the fact that references to this state appear in both his sacred and his secular and in his early and late poetry, and in his prose as well. The classical translations printed in *Olor Iscanus* and *Thalia Rediviva* prove that Vaughan's interest in the "happy state" antedated his conversion and that without strain he was able to move back and forth between the physical and spiritual facets of an idea in which sacred and secular are inextricably blended:

> Who gives the warm Spring temp'rate houres
> Decking the Earth with spicie flowres,
> Or how it Comes (for mans recruit)
> That Autumne yeelds both Grape and fruit,
> With many other Secrets, he
> Could shew the Cause and Mysterie.
>   But now that light is almost out,
> And the brave Soule lyes Chain'd about
> With outward Cares, whose pensive weight
> Sinks down her Eyes from their first height,
> And clean Contrary to her birth
> Poares on this vile and foolish Earth (p. 77).

In the translations from Boethius we see the first traces of such characteristic themes as the impermanence of human affairs, the corrupting complexity of modern life, and the power of love. Boethius also provided Vaughan with the structural pattern of one of his most famous paradisal poems. Compare, on this point, "The Retreate" with Vaughan's translation of Metrum V, Book 2, of Boethius's *Consolation:*

Happy that first white age! when wee	Happy those early dayes! when I
Lived by the Earths meere Charitie,	Shin'd in my Angell-infancy;
No soft luxurious Diet then	
Had Effeminated men,	
No other meat, nor wine had any	
Then the Course Mast, or simple honey,	

And by the Parents care layd
    up
Cheap *Berries* did the Children
    sup
     * * * * * * * * *

No stirring Drum had scarr'd
    that age,
Nor the shrill Trumpets active
    rage,
No wounds by bitter hatred
    made
With warm bloud soil'd the
    shining blade;
For how could hostile madness
    arm
An age of love to publick harm?
When Common Justice none
    withstood,
Nor sought rewards for spilling
    bloud.
  O that at length our age
    would raise
Into the temper of those dayes!
    * * * * * * * * *

Alas! who was it that first
    found
Gold hid of purpose under
    ground,
That sought out Pearles, and
    div'd to find
Such pretious perils for man-
    kind! (p. 83).

Before I taught my tongue to
    wound
My Conscience with a sinfull
    sound,
Or had the black art to dis-
    pence
A sev'rall sin to ev'ry sence,

But felt through all this fleshly
    dresse
Bright *shootes* of everlasting-
    nesse.
  O how I long to travell back
And tread again that ancient
    track!
    * * * * * * * * *

But (ah!) my soul with too
    much stay
Is drunk, and staggers in the
    way.
Some men a forward motion
    love,
But I by backward steps would
    move,
And when this dust falls to the
    urn
In that state I came return (pp.
    419–420).

Vaughan borrowed not only from Herbert. He borrowed from himself as well! For the paradisal motif Vaughan is indebted also to Vergil, Ovid, Ausonius, and the Polish Jesuit Casimirus. That great medieval symbol of rebirth, the phoenix, finds its way into Vaughan through a translation of a poem by Claudian. In a translation from Anselm, *Man in Glory*, Vaughan cultivates primarily the spiritual blessings of Paradise—wisdom, peace, security, and joy, not neglecting, however, such earthly gifts as beauty, strength, liberty, health, pleasure, friendship, and "a sufficiency, or fulnesse of all good things, according to our own desire, and without any indigency" (p. 209). The happiest of all confusions of the good things of this life with the good things of heaven appears in Vaughan's translation of Guevara's *The Praise and Happiness of the Country Life:*

O who can ever fully expresse the pleasures and happinesse of the Country-life! with the various and delightfull sports of *fishing, hunting* and *fowling,* with *guns, Greyhounds, Spaniels,* and severall sorts of *Nets!* what oblectation and refreshment it is, to behold the *green shades,* the beauty and Majestie of the tall and antient *groves,* to be skill'd in *planting* and dressing of *Orchards, Flowres* and *Pot-Herbs,* to temper and allay these harmlesse *imployments* with some innocent merry *song,* to ascend sometimes to the *fresh* and *healthfull hils,* to descend into the *bosome* of the *valleys,* and the fragrant, deawy *meadows,* to heare the *musick* of *birds,* the *murmurs* of *Bees,* the *falling* of *springs,* and the pleasant discourses of the *Old Plough-men,* where without any impediment or trouble a man may walk, and, (as *Cato Censorius* us'd to say) discourse with the *dead,* that is read the pious works of learned men who departing this life left behind them their *noble thoughts,* for the benefit of *posterity,* and the preservation of their own worthy *names* (p. 130).

In writing about Paradise, Vaughan created some of his most striking and characteristic images. One well-known and frequently employed symbol is *light*, an entirely appropriate symbol for divine grace and a word whose Welsh equivalent, *gwyn*, means, Hutchinson points out, all that is "fair, happy, holy, and blessed" and forms the basis for *gywnfyd*, "white world," the Welsh word for Paradise.[15] It is not easy to determine what exactly was Vaughan's experience with light, for I am not at all sure that he ever enjoyed the mystical experience which Evelyn Underhill has described as "a flooding of the personality with new light." Vaughan's lines are too full of the fiery torments of judgment day to be wholly effective as statements of the mystical experience, and he is not above such grotesque, Crashavian images as the star pearled with tears. Even his greatest light images—the "great *Ring* of pure and endless light"—are, like so many of Dante's images, extremely difficult to localize among the senses or involve a transfer of perceptions from one sense organ to another (synaesthesia). This common feature of mystic poetry is apparent in lines from "The Rainbow":

> How bright wert thou, when *Shems* admiring eye
> Thy burnisht, flaming *Arch* did first descry!
> When *Terah, Nahor, Haran, Abram, Lot,*
> The youthful world's gray fathers in one knot,
> Did with intentive looks watch every hour
> For thy new light, and trembled at each shower!
> When thou dost shine darkness looks white and fair,
> Storms turn to Musick, clouds to smiles and air:
> Rain gently spends his honey-drops, and pours
> Balm on the cleft earth, milk on grass and flowers (p. 509).

Nevertheless, Vaughan can suggest with telling deftness and

absolute precision the flashing quality of light darting among shadows:

> The unthrift Sunne shot vitall gold
>   A thousand peeces,
> And heaven its azure did unfold
>   Checqur'd with snowie fleeces (p. 398),

and also, through the awesome brilliance of the comet or the rainbow, the idea that light means sudden, apocalyptic revelation:

> The whole Creation shakes off night,
> And for thy shadow looks the light,
> Stars now vanish without number,
> Sleepie Planets set, and slumber,
> The pursie Clouds disband, and scatter,
> All expect some sudden matter,
> Not one beam triumphs, but from far
>   That morning-star (p. 452).

The shift from these tender, naive lines to the magnificent images of "Ascension Day" suggests how really varied Vaughan's sensitivity to light could be:

> When Heav'n above them shin'd like molten glass,
> When all the Planets did unclouded pass (p. 482).

In treatment of light, Vaughan's only master in English literature is Jeremy Taylor. In the realm of painting, comparisons with the work of Georges LaTour are suggested.

There is a flurry of suggestive paradisal images in "Son-Dayes"—the hills of myrrh, love feasts, honeycombs, the Milky Way—all rich, if overly "pretty," analogues of spiritual happiness. More important images—images which suggest Vaughan's power to pick out of his environment just what he needed for his purposes—are found in wind and rain ("Rain gently spends his honey-drops"), in the dawn, in the fermentation of wine, in the waking of a silken butterfly. The sap which rises in the tree, the thought of his brother in Heaven repairing "Such losses as befel him in this air" (p. 478), and the harmless violets used for salves and syrups—all become concrete symbols of healing and refreshment. The experience of Paradise may also involve escape, but Vaughan's images of the "young Roe/Upon the mounts of spices" (p. 410) and of being set in flight suggest rather the positive exhilaration of movement than any sense of release from danger. Yet because this is still the world, grave dangers prompt man to flee, healing showers are withheld, light is to be seen only through crannies, and poor men groan to see even the edges of God's "bordering light." Moreover, communion with God is yet to be achieved—

> . . . Angels here
>   Shall yet to man appear,
> And familiarly confer
> Beneath the Oke and Juniper (p. 499).

Thus, as far as man is concerned, the secrets of Paradise, though glimpsed, are not yet really out. It is impossible to determine whether Vaughan at this point found his vision growing obscure, or whether he turned his back on his responsibilities as a visionary poet to see as deeply and as widely as possible, or whether he was simply overwhelmed by a love for the esoteric and felt it impossible to advance to deeper insights.

In a remarkable passage from his *Apology for Liturgy*, Jeremy Taylor argues that the Church of England is constituted so as to supply all human spiritual needs: there are forms of confession for the contrite soul, and forms of thanksgiving; there are prayers which express the needs of the community and prayers for the earnest and fervent individual; all anniversaries both public and private are recognized. It is inconceivable, he feels, that any spiritual blessing could be imagined for which provision is not made. Despite Taylor's appeal to "interior acts and forms of worship," it is evident that he was expressing an essentially objective— indeed aristocratic—point of view, an attitude directed toward the preservation of a body of practices shared and honored by the entire community. To more evangelically-minded believers, much of what Taylor boasted about must have seemed largely irrelevant, the essence of religion being less the preservation or celebration of something that is possessed than a continuing movement toward something still to be won; less, again, something held by the entire community; more something found by every man in his own heart. In a situation where yesterday's victories may be quickly wiped out or proven vain, traveling, going on pilgrimage becomes inevitable; darkness, the condition; some distant light, the goal; some warmth in the heart, the promise of future blessing. The evangelical stress on the very personal relationship between Christ and the believer, frustrated and yet full of hope, was never better put than in Vaughan's "Love-Sick":

Iesus, my life! how shall I truly love thee?
O that thy Spirit would so strongly move me,

That thou wert pleas'd to shed thy grace so farr
As to make man all pure love, flesh a star!
A star that would ne'r set, but ever rise,
So rise and run, as to out-run these skies,
These narrow skies (narrow to me) that barre,
So barre me in, that I am still at warre,
At constant warre with them. O come and rend,
Or bow the heavens! Lord bow them and descend,
And at thy presence make these mountains flow,
These mountains of cold Ice in me! Thou art
Refining fire, O then refine my heart,
My foul, foul heart! Thou art immortall heat,
Heat motion gives; Then warm it, till it beat,
So beat for thee, till thou in mercy hear,
So hear that thou must open: open to
A sinfull wretch, A wretch that caus'd thy woe,
Thy woe, who caus'd his weal; so far his weal
That thou forgott'st thine own, for thou didst seal
Mine with thy blood, thy blood which makes thee mine,
Mine ever, ever; And me ever thine (page 493).

Any estimate of gains or losses sustained through the point
of view represented by Vaughan would have to embrace a
number of strengths and weaknesses—the tendency of poems
like this one to lose their intellectual bearings and deteriorate
into a series of weak, paradoxical ejaculations; the vagaries
of subjectivism particularly as they have been laid bare by
critics like Irving Babbitt; the contention of men who have
taken the other side and have insisted that the heart's deter-
minations alone matter; the fact that Vaughan's voice was
pretty well lost for two hundred years and that it is hardly a
strong one today; the further fact that the Anglican communion—powerful in the 17th century—has lost ground
heavily in modern times because its communal sense was not

nearly inclusive enough; and the frequent tendency of evangelical piety to become a series of cold, scholastic rigidities.
It seems as difficult to make some final determination here as
it is in the age-old debate between Romanticism and Classicism.

But these are issues which will come up inevitably when,
as Vaughan did, a man gives his external allegiance to one
master and permits his heart to be wooed by another. This
chapter has not attempted to advance the argument that
Anglicanism in the 17th century was a purely objective
creed which left no room for warmth and emotion, or that
evangelical piety was essentially subjective (Calvin was certainly a master of the most important facts—social and intellectual—of his world). Nor has the view presented here
been that inner-directedness is necessarily superior (for a
poet) to an exclusive outer-directedness, nor, least of all, that
Vaughan was insincere. But it must be admitted that
Vaughan wrote within a tradition which of all the non-Roman
creeds is the most objectively, the most communally oriented.
His church deeply needed the sweetness and grace of
Vaughan's inner dialogue with God, the earnestness of his
search for Paradise. But as he pursued these values, Vaughan
lost the nourishment which the English communion might
have provided for him. Vaughan chose to form his experience
out of personal emotional responses, elemental impulses,
visions, and the paraphernalia of daily rural life. His ordering of experience is effective as it comes from his pen, but it
has not always proven easy to sustain or to communicate.
Moreover, it did not embrace a very significant segment of
the most stimulating ideas of the 17th century; it was, even
in Vaughan's own age, a muted voice, the voice of a minor

poet. Curious, is it not, that seeking Paradise should be—poetically at least—so much more of a minor task than losing it!

Jeremy Taylor: theology and aesthetics

5

I. "What Think Ye of Christ?"

The last two chapters have been concerned with problems of artistic and intellectual adjustment: we have seen the whole response of a poet caught up in a single great metaphor and a man of science frustrated in his attempt to penetrate into other modes of being by rationalistic tendencies which would not allow natural processes to operate. Sometimes, the most hopeful attempts at adjustment, accommodation, and harmonization run into barriers and snags that seem insuperable. The divine is tormented by the flesh or fascinated by intellectual paradox; the philosopher lacks the power to make others listen to his voice; the man of faith finds one article of the creed always catching in his throat; the encyclopedic poet finds himself shut off from books; the city lover is doomed to live in the country; the gentle dreamer, in a time of wars and tumult. These frustrations make interesting material for biographers. In the ways they have been surmounted or avoided there lies, too, a fascinating record of human ingenuity, imagination, and improvisation.

The particular problem under discussion here is the challenge offered to the liberal theologian by the old gospel question, "What think ye of Christ?" Here is an issue that has inspired instances of unimaginable human cruelty or induced in sincere men (who cannot at the cost of all their integrity affirm what they do not really believe) the gravest anguish. Few people in our generation are able to comprehend the depth of meaning this question has had for earlier generations or can see how much was hanging on the kind of answer that was given. One characteristic response was that offered by John Milton in *Paradise Lost:*

> Thou therefore whom thou only canst redeem,
> Their Nature also to thy Nature join;
> And be thyself Man among men on Earth,
> Made flesh, when time shall be, of Virgin seed,
> By wondrous birth: Be thou in *Adam's* room
> The Head of all mankind, though *Adam's* Son.
> As in him perish all men, so in thee
> As from a second root shall be restor'd,
> As many as are restor'd, without thee none (III, 281–289).

These observations by "th'Almighty" have probably gone a long way toward suggesting that Milton, like so many others

of his age, found it hard to warm to questions of Christology.
Quite another tack was taken by Giles Fletcher in touching,
melting words from *Christ's Victory and Triumph:*

> He is a path, if any be misled;
> He is a robe, if any naked be;
> If any chance to hunger, He is bread;
> If any be a bondman, He is free:
>   To dead men life He is, to sick men health;
>   To blind men sight, and to the needy wealth—
> A pleasure without loss, a treasure without stealth.

There is a world of difference between the intellectual
answer proposed by Milton and Fletcher's appeal to simple,
trusting piety. I should say that one most important contrast lies in the nature of the *power* being offered. Few
casual readers of the two passages would hesitate long over
a choice, for the appeal of Fletcher is to the most basic
human needs: Christ offers a way, clothing, bread, freedom,
life, recovery—indeed, every resource necessary for man. In
its pathos, the appeal is irresistible. It is more difficult to
appreciate what Milton found in Christ—the power that
comes from comprehending certain fundamental relationships—the link between the divine and the human, between
flesh and spirit, between one man and all men; and a comprehension of the nature of growth and renewal. Yet these
were really the crucial issues for 17th century religious
thinkers (as they are for us), and they were issues which
had to be faced if faith was to remain a relevant part of the
intellectual life of the age. The situation might be compared
to the way the early Church had to resolve the problem of the
place of Christ in the Godhead, or St. Anselm had to explain

why God became man, or the 20th century has had to deal
with Christ's relationship to his own age and to the Church.

The 17th century, however, was less interested in Christ's
relationship with the Church than in the nature of the
Church itself, so that serious inquiries into the fundamental
problems of Christology were rare. One of the few attempts
to grapple with the problem was made by Jeremy Taylor in
his devotional biography, *The Great Exemplar,* and even it
must be seen as a "popular" rather than a "scholarly" work.
Taylor published this book in 1649, two years after he had
grappled with the problems of the larger world in *The Liberty of Prophesying,* and just before he wrote *Holy Living*
and *Holy Dying,* the books on which much of his fame rests.
Five years later, with *The Real Presence,* Taylor embarked
on the seas of controversy. We see him in 1649 not warring
but seeking to accommodate, not troubling the waters and,
therefore, not yet being accused of heresy. Indeed, in the pro-
nouncements that he made throughout his life, a solid base
of orthodox and acceptable opinion can be seen: Taylor always maintained a wholehearted belief in the necessity of
scriptural revelation; he put a proper stress on the place of
the will in determining the sinfulness or innocence of action;
and he had, in *The Liberty of Prophesying,* defined the doctrine of Christ crucified as "the great and entire complexion
of a Christian's faith." [1] On the other hand, certain views
that were later to cause him much trouble were doubtless
being formed even this early. In *Holy Dying* Taylor was to
manifest a pessimism about the state of man which at first
glance seems more Calvinist than Anglican, but which is
actually frankly humanistic and not theological at all. Taylor's thinking about the problem of sin, as he puts it down in

the notorious eighth chapter of *Unum Necessarium*, was that
it was not original, not inherent, only imputed to man, and
that it constituted a stain, not a damning indictment. The
evil of the human situation is not to be explained theologically, suggests Taylor, but on the basis of psychological and
cultural determinants—the decay of the times, the entangled
state of human affairs, the weaknesses and infirmities which
stem from our inadequate brains and senses.

Clearly, Taylor's sympathies lay with the camp of the lib-
erals and the nonintellectuals (groups that do not always
bivouac together), with those for whom a systematic statement about Christ meant less than the attempt to make
Christ relevant to the simple needs of human beings. In *The
Real Presence* he declares, "The natural eating of Christ's
flesh . . . alone and of itself does no good, does not give
life; but the spiritual eating of Him is the instrument of life
to us" (VI, 32). From such a position, Taylor's theology
of the atonement developed quite naturally: Christ saves
us, he declares,

not only by procuring pardon for them [our sins], but by turning
us from our iniquities, by efforming us anew, by reforming whatsoever was amiss in manners and persuasion, by conforming us
to the similitude of the holiness and perfections of God. . . . [He]
never leaves us till our graces are perfect and even with eternal
felicities (IX, 475).

Besides making Christ little more than an ethical model,
Taylor pushes agnosticism to the very limits that the Christian faith will bear, to a place where doubts arise about the
possibility of man's knowing final truth, either here or ultimately. There is in Taylor, too, a considerably stronger

stress on reason than is entirely consonant with the Christian position: faith must be supported, Taylor declares, by each individual's personal judgment of the validity of revelation. Reason, moreover, establishes the grounds of faith in God, clarifies Scripture, and prompts ethical action. Evaluating the meaning of these stands is difficult: the problem of Taylor's Christology, for example, is not so much that it is heretical as that it is indifferent to much that has been found important in the Christian tradition. Coleridge explained Taylor's case with perhaps too much vigor:

The truth is Taylor was a Pelagian, believed that without Christ thousands, Jews and heathen, lived wisely and holily, and went to heaven; but this he did not dare to say out, probably not even to himself; and hence it is that he founders backward and forward, now upping and now downing.[2]

It is not difficult to see why this problem of defining the significance of Christ was so important for Taylor. Sheldon, an opponent since Taylor's days as a student, had declared him "a man of dangerous tempers, apt to break out into extravagances," [3] and Sheldon was speaking for a tradition that regarded the doctrine of the incarnation as the *unum neces-sarium,* the fundamental dogma about which there could be no debate. With the publication in 1624 of Lord Herbert of Cherbury's *De Veritate,* a neglect, or slighting, of the atonement became a hallmark of natural theology, or deism, and this fact was surely not lost on Taylor's opponents. By 1649, too, Taylor had lost his great and (theologically) liberal patron Laud; his future may well have depended on a statement about Christ that would satisfy the orthodox. This was no manufactured need, and certainly it is not my intention to condemn Taylor for the line he took. He wanted a concept of Christ that would bear fruit in holy lives and discourage controversy, and to achieve this goal he felt compelled to avoid all but the simplest theoretical formulations. In neglecting to establish a firm intellectual basis for his thinking, however, he seriously limited the influence of his book. The importance of a clear and rigorous theory in these areas is indicated by the productive activity within the Christian Church today—activity springing from frank discussion of the problem of Christology—the very issue Taylor felt compelled to skirt.

II. Toward an answer

Taylor found help in several places. There were resources in the intellectual and aesthetic climate of his day which rendered the problem less agonizing than it might have been for a modern liberal in Taylor's position. There was a long tradition of medieval books about Christ which side-stepped theological issues in order to concentrate on the nurturing of personal piety. And there was a comprehensive art style—the Baroque—which Taylor found both personally pleasing as well as appropriate for the presentation of the story of Jesus. Taylor's *Great Exemplar* is thus an example of an interesting phenomenon—the employment of a literary form or an artistic style not merely to please or to illustrate but as a means of actually resolving an intellectual problem. Taylor's work might therefore be compared to the claim of Frank Lloyd Wright that his designs for buildings and cities would force broad new patterns of life upon those who lived in them. The pastoral tradition within which Milton wrote "Lycidas" seems to have provided the poet with a pattern of response to experience which helped him in the solution of personal difficulties. And within the form of the Mass, Bach apparently found the artistic inspiration to transcend both the Catholic and the Protestant traditions. Style, it has been said, is power, but quite a different kind of power from that supplied by the intellect. A style, such as the curt, may permit ideas to be expressed with maximum clarity, or it may, as the Ciceronian does, convey a feeling of assurance or affirmation. The recessional style about which Wölfflin talks may indicate the presence in Rembrandt of some mystery and the atechtonic style may imply uncertainty or confusion.[4] But it belongs to the power of the intellect to elucidate the idea, to explain the relationship which is being affirmed, to identify the mystery, and to resolve the uncertainty. This is why I contend, in this paper, that Taylor, in his book on Christ and by his heavy reliance on style in his presentation, was skirting rather that grappling with the really important issues.

But to pick up other important issues dropped at the middle of the last paragraph, I suggested that there were, first of all, some currents in the 17th century that helped Taylor to neutralize the difficulties in which he found himself. He was fortunate, for example, that none of the confusions generated in the 20th century by fundamentalism, literalism, mythicism, and irrationalism were present as irritants on the scene which he knew. Some of these problems were eliminated at the start by firm social distinctions which linked the evangelical line with the scorned and ill-trained mechanic-preachers and the love of reason and traditional learning with the Establishment and the universities. Seventeenth-century thinking about Jesus was untouched by the kind of scepticism about the Biblical record which has resulted from modern scholarship and which sent Schweitzer and Bultmann off on their study of the historical Jesus. There was not in the 17th century the dead weight of apathy and hostility that led Matthew Arnold to attempt an interpretation of the Christian faith that would be relevant to his age, nor was there much danger from the uncritical idealism that prompted 19th century poets to see in Christ the highest type of humanity. Christian ethics, still bound to casuistry, the Church fathers, and scholastic theology, had not yet begun to examine critically the Gospel commands, so that phrases like "divine imperative," "interim ethic," and "de-mythologizing" were not troubling the waters. Indeed, it is not easy to imagine an area of scholarship that has ever been quite so moribund as Christology was in this age, or more dependent for its revitalization on certain intellectual insights that had not been attained. These deficiencies worked to Taylor's advantage, however, since the main negative element which he had to face was the orthodoxy of his age. But even this was tempered by the willingness of many of his contemporaries to admit diverse opinions, their desire to maintain balance and moderation, their refusal to grant to any man or group the privilege of infallibility, and a certain degree of pragmatism which encouraged the question, "How does the acceptance of the dogma of the Atonement work out in practice?" [5]

Another significant element in the intellectual climate of the day was a widespread sympathy throughout the Anglican communion for natural theology, a point of view which appealed to Taylor as well. Thus when he is trying to show that Christianity heightens rather than diminishes the measure of happiness which men enjoy, Taylor observes that Christianity employs for its purposes all the human appetites. Erotic love, by which men propagate families, is seen as an imitation or reflection of the love owed to God. The woman at the well in Samaria was quick to allow Christ to transform her hunger —unsatisfied by many husbands—into a desire for God, so that her lust became charity. There is, in Taylor's thinking, no justification for the human tendency to find natural weaknesses an insuperable handicap to piety. Rather, if men live according to their basic desires and intuitions, they will live reasonably and virtuously. Within such a scheme, which maintains that man has in himself what he needs for salvation, there can be little place for either grace or faith. Taylor, impatient of both extremity and irrationality, describes faith as a kind of natural prompting, independent of reason and yet working with it. He observes that even such severe Christian virtues as humility and celibacy—virtues practiced only where there is belief in a divine moral order—have had a long history in human affairs. They far antedate the New Testament, he insists, and grow out of certain natural human propensities. Indeed, virtue is pursued even into subhuman species: what men do in faith or through understanding, animals do out of the natural wisdom of instinct. In the realm of morality, this position leads Taylor to a vigorous condemnation of casuistry, which seeks to measure the number of gestures which will please God: the natural response of the heart to God is a surer guide to what will be pleasing to God than are the calculations of the mind. Ultimately Taylor is driven to the pragmatic conclusion that Christ can be imitated by human beings and, indeed, that holy living is far less trouble than profane living.

Thus even the piety which Taylor envisions is a natural movement of the soul. By following Christ, he says he means no ridiculous kind of imitation, nothing "fantastic or impertinent" (II, 40), none of the extreme forms of piety which might elicit grace from God by force. Rather, he insists, the means of worship ought to be as simple and natural as the piety itself—an imitation of the human acts of Christ, a reaction to life patterned on what is known of His responses, a quality of life that is as gracious as it is natural:

He that gives alms to the poor, takes Jesus by the hand; he that patiently endures injuries and affronts, helps Him to bear His cross; he that comforts his brother in affliction, gives an amiable kiss of peace to Jesus; he that bathes his own and his neighbours' sins in tears of penance and compassion, washes his master's feet: we lead Jesus into the recesses of our heart by holy meditations; and we enter into His heart, when we express Him in our actions: for so the apostle says, "he that is in Christ, walks as He also walked" (II, 46).

Such a statement as to what man may make of Christ has more virtue as a moving compromise than as an adequate, intellectual description of who Christ was in all His fullness. But there can be little doubt, I think, that we keep difficulties alive sometimes when we insist on solving them within one specific framework. Valuable, for instance, as the concept of God's "wholly otherness" has been, it has tended to render many theological problems impenetrable to the kind of intellectual debate with which men sometimes effectively attack other areas of difficulty. Taylor's interest in what man makes of God, rather than in what God makes of man, is exactly what might be expected of a humanist, and when he possesses the artistic skill to make this view convincing, he succeeds, I believe, in making a fresh and suggestive approach to this problem and perhaps to some others.

Another source of help for Taylor—over and beyond the religious temper of his age which admitted the testimony of natural theology—was a long literary tradition, going back to the Middle Ages, of devotional books that centered their attention upon the life of Christ. Edmund Gosse, in his biography of Taylor for the English Men of Letters series, mistakenly called *The Great Exemplar* the first modern life of Christ. But those who open the book expecting something like the books of Renan, Francis Burkitt, or Shirley Jackson Case will be confused. In form, at least, Taylor's book resembles much more closely the medieval or Renaissance devotional guide, a genre embracing a host of uncompromisingly serious volumes. Thomas à Kempis's *Imitation of Christ* is perhaps the best known modern survivor of this form, but less well known volumes, like Becon's *Sicke Man's Salve* (1561), Hieron's *A Helpe unto Devotion* (8th edition, 1616), and Bayly's *The Practice of Pietie* (3rd edition, 1613),[6] all accomplished the general purposes of the meditation—warning and comforting, encouraging prayer and imitation of Christ, guiding the believer toward holy thoughts. So large, indeed, is the number of titles that it is possible to distinguish highly specialized types among them, in many of which Taylor worked. The guide to public prayer, for example, was a distinct form, represented by Taylor's *Collection of Offices* (1659), which he prepared when the Book of Common Prayer was proscribed by the Puritans. More personal prayers were collected in *The Golden Grove,* a book belonging to a type which has been traced back to St. Augustine down through the penitential writings of St. Bernard and Thomas à Kempis, to the 17th century writings of Andrewes, Ken, Becon, Hieron, and Henry Bull. It is customary, in treating Renaissance books of private devotion, to distinguish between the so-called psalters (based primarily on selections from the Psalms, with special added prayers), and the primers, which employ a greater variety of Biblical material, from both Old and New Testaments, adding much by way of comment and meditation. The beautiful Protestant Primer issued by Redman in 1535 included selections from the Life of Christ and the Passion, comments on the Lord's Prayer and the Ten Commandments, as well as a selection of original prayers. This book and its successors [7] resemble closely what Taylor was to do over a century later. *The Great Exemplar,* with its pronounced concern for the common experiences of life—affliction, childbirth, soldiering, travel, human affection—is generally Protestant in its outlook; other volumes, like Ken's, were prepared for some special audience; still others were decidedly Roman in the way they followed the liturgical year and the ecclesiastical hours.

Taylor's two most famous books, *Holy Living* and *Holy Dying,* belong to still other traditions of devotional writing —books on conduct and books on the art of dying. Of greater relevance to present concerns, however, is the life-of-Christ genre, and it is to this medieval type of devotional book, rather than to the modern tradition of critical biography that Taylor's book belongs. Almost as soon as *The Great Exemplar* was published, Taylor's debt to the *Vita Christi* by Ludolphus of Saxony (who died in 1378) was recognized.

Indeed, Taylor was accused of plagiarism by John Serjeant, a Catholic controversialist. Ludolphus's book has been described as a harmonization of the four gospel accounts of the life of Christ with commentary from medieval and patristic writings. Prayers at the end of each section set forth "the quintessence of the author's devout meditations." [8] Actually Taylor makes little pretense at originality, for he refers conspicuously in *Holy Dying* to still another devotional biography, a work of the school of Bonaventura translated in the 15th Century by Nicholas Love. The Love-Bonaventura work includes prayers and exhortations to personal spiritual development and is in part narration, in part meditation.

In books like these, Taylor found the form he needed, one which would permit him to retell either briefly or at length the gospel stories which moved him deeply or not at all. Moreover, he had here a form which made possible the inclusion of extended essays on ethical topics suggested by the New Testament narrative and prayers for those who were using the book as a devotional guide. The barest statistics will show how freely Taylor departed from pure narrative to include other kinds of material: a total of eighty-eight pages in the Eden-Heber edition are devoted to gospel narrative, no segment being longer than three pages, with prayers of about twenty-five lines apiece at the end of each section. On the other hand, the discourses and "considerations" run to as many as forty pages apiece. Such variety, Taylor confesses, is the essence of his scheme, for the book is so dressed that some parts will "satisfy our discourse" (i.e., the intelligence or the dialectic faculty in man); some parts, our affections; and all "relate to practice" (II, 34). Taylor's medieval models rendered the historical facts about Christ of little more importance than they had been to St. John: Taylor was not weighing the facts of history or trying to re-create the life and times of Jesus or walk where He walked. Rather, his goal was to put the traditional figure of Christ into a certain artistic framework where It could be contemplated, thereby touching the lives of those who gazed upon It. The thinking behind this approach to piety seems not unlike the psychology of the passions, which was receiving so much attention at this time.

Taylor's concern with the effect of his narrative is to be seen in his discussion of the function of the "meditation," a statement that grows directly out of the essentially medieval form which he was employing and out of his conviction that natural man could work out his own salvation. Admitting regretfully that the art of meditation is as unaccustomed to our dry souls as "the undiscovered treasures of the Indian hills" (II, 129), he nevertheless insists that it is a mental discipline that can be practiced, since it employs all those "arguments, motives, and irradiations which God intended to be instrumental to piety." Thus, piety and devotion are again found to be completely natural to man. Based solidly on man's imaginative and intellectual powers (the "rational soul"), meditation is nevertheless directed beyond these to what Taylor calls spiritual understanding, which is concerned with the soul in its future state of glory. This faculty must in turn be illumined by the imagination, since understanding alone can make religion "lasting and reasonable" (II, p. 325), but it is the work of fancy to make religion "scrupulous, strict, operative, and effectual." Here again we are driven to a recognition of the place of art and style in the religious life, a position which is strengthened by Taylor's own insistence that meditation ought to be concerned with concrete and vivid objects:

Holy meditation produces the passions and desires it intends; it makes the object present and almost sensible: it renews the first passions by a fiction of imagination; it passes from the paschal parlour to Cedron, it tells the drops of sweat, and measures them, and finds them as big as drops of blood, and then conjectures at the greatness of our sins; it fears in the midst of Christ's agonies, it hears His groans, it spies Judas' lantern afar off, it follows Jesus to Gabbatha, and wonders at His innocence and their malice, and feels the strokes of the whip, and shrinks the head, when the crown of thorns is thrust hard upon His holy brows; and at last goes step by step with Jesus, and carries part of the cross, and is nailed fast with sorrow and compassion, and dies with love (II, 133–134).

Indeed, all the advice that Taylor gives about the art of meditation—the consideration of plain propositions rather than speculation, putting decisions and insights into immediate action, and the refusal to abandon a stream of thought until some benefit is derived from it—all suggest the characteristically Taylorian emphasis on the practical rather than the speculative, on that which tends to virtue rather than on the purely intellectual or even the purely emotional. I wonder whether Taylor ever really grasped the spirit of many of these older texts. It is true that in describing the illuminative way he follows the medieval pattern, and that in talking about the unitive way he comes close to an experiential description of mysticism: it is, he says,

a prayer of quietness and silence, and a meditation extraordinary, a discourse without variety, a vision and intuition of divine ex-

cellencies, an immediate entry into an orb of light, and a resolution of all our faculties into sweetnesses, affections, and starings
upon the divine beauty (II, 139).

But all that is known about Taylor's stress on rational intelligence, his intellectual prejudices, and his activism forces us
to look with some suspicion on statements like this. To sit in
absolute quietness of mind and to let the Holy Spirit speak
was foreign to Taylor's mode of acting, as was the idea of
any kind of mystical union in which the rational mind might
have to assume a subordinate role.[9] Taylor inherited a form
for his thinking which had a limited but genuine usefulness
for him: it provided practice in the use of the imagination
and it gave him a structure on which to project his own essentially aesthetic appreciation of Christ, in a style provided by
his own century.

III. A baroque life of Christ

An important part of the aesthetic impression made by *The
Great Exemplar* is the sheer massiveness of the text—its
seven hundred odd pages crammed with narrative and speculative matter and with images of unremitting grandeur and
pathos making it one of the most impressive of all devotional
guides. The richness which Taylor achieved suggests, once
again, that he was trying to resolve his intellectual problem
by transferring it to the realm of the emotions where other
forces could be brought to bear upon it. This approach, of
course, is to be seen in everything Taylor wrote, and it jus-
tifies Hallam's remark that Taylor was the "first who

sapped and shook the foundations of dogmatism and pre-
tended orthodoxy; the first who taught men to seek peace in
unity of spirit rather than of belief; and, instead of extin-
guishing dissent, to take away its sting by charity, and by a
sense of humility." [10] Thus we find Taylor in this long book
not concerned with broaching or supporting heresies but attempting to draw out of the story of Christ every human
appeal that he can find. In *The Great Exemplar* he did not
err about Christ's divinity or His manhood or their conjunc-
tion; he simply chose not to make these issues relevant. His
own discussion of the phrase, *hoc est corpus meum,* reveals
his preoccupation: it is, he declares, a *tropical* question, with
"est" being used because in Aramaic there was no "signifi-
cat." But does the trope, he wonders, lie in "est" or in
"corpus?" His interest in Hebrew and Syriac grammar and in
rhetorical niceties far surpasses his interest in Christology.
Doubtless Taylor's superiors would have welcomed a precise
theological statement about his views on Christ, and, indeed,
in all cases where a problem demands the demonstration of
cause, effect, definition, anaylsis, or prediction, nothing will
serve but clear thought. But if the problem can be made one
of structuring or arrangement of parts, of distancing or relat-
ing, art—whether poetry, painting, or music—is often as
useful a way of problem resolving as word or concept. Taylor
solved his problem by retelling the life of Christ in such a
way that the very manner of presentation suggested the appropriate response of the believer. Thus, he established a
relationship between man and God that was comprehensible
on human terms.

Sometimes, we know from his other books, this relationship demanded from man some response of the believing

mind, sometimes an act of practical piety, sometimes the stirring of an emotion such as joy or sorrow or awe. All of these demands which religion may make upon a man are exercised and encouraged by Taylor's life of Christ: discourses on moral and theological topics arouse the mind, recitations of the good deeds of Christ stir thoughts of imitation, the grandeur of the book's conception creates a sense of awe and magnificence, and the pathos of many of the details is clearly designed to encourage a sense of intimate relationship between the believer and Christ. This pathos emerges in part from Taylor's concentration upon the birth and death of Christ, in part from any number of quiet observations that he makes—like his comment that God guides men whose lives are holy "as He does little birds to make rare nests, though they understand not the mystery of operation, nor the design and purpose of the action" (II, 286). Other leading motifs in *The Great Exemplar* can also be explained by reference to Baroque psychology—the stress on light and color, the persistent images of swelling and overflowing, and the spirit of elevation that suffuses the whole. "Baroque" is by this time an ambiguous and somewhat awkward term, borrowed as it was originally from painting and architecture, and it is not especially popular today in any field. But the effect of Taylor's book is much like that left by certain massive 17th century churches and by the paintings of Rembrandt, Rubens, and Poussin, and I have little doubt that Taylor created his effects with as much deliberation as any painter: the towering, statuesque massiveness to eliminate all danger of "enthusiasm," and a highly stylized pathos to offset any purely speculative or intellectual approach to a story which Taylor felt to be incomparably rich in human emotional values. Unhappy as the term "Baroque" may be, it describes the impact of Taylor's book remarkably well. Moreover, it reinforces my thesis that Taylor's approach to his problem was a fundamentally aesthetic one—an approach closer to painting or sculpture than to theology.[11]

When we get beyond the sheer size of *The Great Exemplar,* we will probably notice next how carefully Taylor has concentrated on certain parts of the Gospel and has avoided other parts. His favorite passages, quite obviously, are those which describe the great festivals of the church year—Easter and Christmas, the times of the greatest joy and the greatest sadness that men can know. What he does with the Nativity story is quite characteristic of his method. He begins with a description of Christ's conception, suggesting in long periodic sentences the vast stretches of time throughout which Christ was expected. The tumult stirred up in Mary's heart as God and man meet within her is described at some length, and Taylor is not above a theological pun when he describes the ecstatic meeting of Mary and Elizabeth, those two women "pregnant and big with religion" (II, 57). Throughout his discussion of the decree of Herod, the arrival at Bethlehem, and the birth, Taylor treats physical details deliberately and unabashedly. There is, for example, in the treatment of the birth itself, a persistent and entirely relevant use of images of breaking forth, a motif common in Baroque art. Moving, too, is Taylor's description of the humble circumstances of Christ's birth:

Jesus was pleased to be born of a poor mother, in a poor place, in a cold winter's night, far from home, amongst strangers, with all the circumstances of humility and poverty. And no man will have cause to complain of his coarse robe, if he remembers the swaddling clothes of this holy Child; nor to be disquieted at his hard bed, when he considers Jesus laid in a manger; nor to be discontented at his thin table, when he calls to mind the King of heaven and earth was fed with a little breast-milk (II, 67).

The appearance of the angels to the shepherds is done with a wonderful sense of rhythmic variety which suggests the Baroque insistence that the most static objects can be made to pulsate with energy: "God himself in poverty, comes in a prejudice to them that love riches, and simplicity is folly to crafty persons" (II, 89). With charming good humor Taylor describes how the angels returned to Heaven "as soon as these blessed choristers had sung their Christmas carol, and taught the church a hymn to put into her offices for ever in the anniversary of this festivity" (II, 83). Something of the pathos of Herod's slaughter of the "pretty sucklings" is caught, but the meaning of this incident to the medieval typologists—these children were the first Christian martyrs —is lost. And, to move for a comparison in the other direction, let Taylor's treatment of the flight to Egypt be compared to a frankly Romantic version—like Merson's "Repose in Egypt," and it will be apparent how little of the mystery inherent in the whole incident Taylor has caught.

In his study of 13th century French art, *The Gothic Image,* Emile Mâle describes a collection of Gospel texts, with illustrations of the events at the beginning and end of Christ's life, but no pictures at all for the events between the Transfiguration and Holy Week. Mâle's observation that this was the normal practice in dealing with the liturgical calendar is confirmed by examination of the paintings of Christ's

life which Giotto did for the Arena Chapel in Padua—a
heavy concentration on the events before and at birth, general neglect of Christ's ministry, and renewed interest in the
scenes of the last days. In Taylor's book the same pattern is
observed. Interest generated by the Nativity clearly flags
when Christ, at twelve, visits the Temple, only to rise again
with treatment of John the Baptist, in whom Taylor sees a
pattern of the "solitary and contemplative life" (II, 164).
The "rite and ceremony" of baptism is handled in a wooden
manner, and the Temptation is awkwardly staged. I recall
no account at all of the Transfiguration, but I remember with
pleasure Taylor's description of the wedding at Cana. Treatment of the miracles is brief, with stress on the charitable
rather than on the supernatural elements. Taylor's attitude
toward the miracles brings to mind Harnack's distinction
between the purely miraculous works (like quieting the
storm) and the more charitable works of mercy.[12] Most of
the account of Christ's ministry is paraphrased from the
Gospels—which suggests that Taylor found these portions
unsuited to the vivid, emotional narrative he was creating.
Nonetheless, even in passages not particularly meaningful
to him personally, his intelligence is at work, separating the
important events from those of lesser meaning, so that the
great light which shines from the earthly ministry of Jesus
might touch all who read.

Taylor begins the third section of *The Great Exemplar*
with a touching account of the response of Mary Magdalen:

She came to Jesus into the pharisee's house: not, as did the staring
multitude, to glut her eyes with the sight of a miraculous and
glorious person; . . . she came in remorse and regret for her sins,

she came to Jesus to lay her burden at His feet, and to present
Him with a broken heart, and a weeping eye, and great affection,
and a box of nard pistic, salutary and precious. For she came
trembling, and fell down before Him, weeping bitterly for her
sins, pouring out a flood great enough to "wash the feet" of the
blessed Jesus, and "wiping them with the hairs of her head"; after
which she "brake the box", and anointed His feet with ointment
(II, 511).

As the narrative moves closer to the last days of Christ's
life, it is enriched with an always moving, frequently un-
earthly style. Sometimes the account is ornate and highly
artistic, as in the description of the way Christ at the tomb
of Lazarus "suffered the passions of piety and humanity, and
wept, distilling that precious liquor into the grave of
Lazarus" (II, 599). Taylor captures effectively the slashing
comments of Christ on the barren fig tree, and the sweetness
and majesty of the funeral sermon, "rarely mixed of sadness
and joys, and studded with mysteries as with emeralds" (II,
607). The account of the last supper itself, however, is as
bare and sparse as a mannerist painting, capturing neither
the psychological interest of da Vinci's painting nor the
sense of mystery of Tintoretto's vast, gloomy, light-smitten
treatment. In quite another spirit is the grim drollery of the
account of Judas's death, in whose bowels burned indignation "with a secret, dark, melancholic fire" (II, 625).
Almost medieval in its blend of timeless detachment and an-
guished feeling is the pietà which Taylor creates as he describes the crucifixion:

By the cross of Christ stood the holy Virgin-mother, upon whom
old Simeon's prophecy was now verified: for now she felt a sword

passing through her very soul: she stood without clamour and womanish noises; sad, silent, and with a modest grief, deep as the waters of the abyss, but smooth as the face of a pool; full of love, and patience, and sorrow, and hope. Now she was put to it to make full use of all those excellent discourses her holy Son had used to build up her spirit, and fortify it against this day. Now she felt the blessings and strengths of faith; and she passed from the griefs of the passion to the expectation of the resurrection; and she rested in this death, as in a sad remedy; for she knew it reconciled God with all the world. But her hope drew a veil before her sorrow; and though her grief was great enough to swallow her up, yet her love was greater, and did swallow up her grief. But the sun also had a veil upon his face, and taught us to draw a curtain before the passion, which would be the most artificial expression of its greatness; whilst by silence and wonder we confess it great beyond our expression, or, which is all one, great as the burden and baseness of our sins. And with this veil drawn before the face of Jesus, let us suppose Him at the gates of paradise, calling with His last words in a loud voice, to have them opened, that "the King of glory might come in" (II, 710).

Lines such as these bring to mind the moving words of Giles Fletcher, which capture, as if in marble, the tender concern of John as he stood by the Cross: "But long he stood, in his faint arms upholding/ The fairest spoil heaven ever forfeited." But neither writer captures the terror of the moment as effectively as Matthias Grunewald's great Crucifixion scene for the Isenheim altar. It is Grunewald's sense of the existentialist terror of the moment which has so impressed modern theologians, and it is such an effect that Taylor is trying hard to avoid, in favor of a monumental Stoicism. Of the biographical account, which ends almost abruptly with the burial and resurrection, little else is worth noting. The humanity of Christ is thus pretty thoroughly neglected—and

with it the mysterious or spiritual. Less important than
Christ's manhood or his divinity was a certain fixed picture
which Taylor had received through tradition. Christ becomes
a symbol, a myth, a participant—to use MacGregor's phrase
—in didactic drama. Such a manipulation was necessary if
Taylor was to solve his problem successfully on an emotional
and aesthetic plane.

It is perhaps uncritical to chide Taylor for omitting this or
that cherished attitude, but even the most generous reader
will be disappointed at missing certain well-loved incidents.
There is, as I have suggested, plenty of pity for the anguish
Christ suffered, but all too little perception of the perfect life
he lived—despite Taylor's central contention that He was the
great exemplar of piety and charity. When a modern critic
like John Baillie speaks of the Gospel story as "the light of
Christian truth which has illumined for me the dark and difficult road of life," [13] he seems to underscore Taylor's failure
to respond in a similarly warm and human fashion. Theologically the book is as weak as one might expect a book
written in lieu of theology to be; morally the book is pedestrian; biographically it is hurried and negligent. This leaves
us with nothing left but the realm of art—Taylor's use of the
Baroque style—as the area within which he faced up to the
problems posed by Christ.

Inherent in many of the events which Taylor chose to retell is that sense of *sursam corda*—lift up your hearts—
which is so characteristic a movement in Baroque art.
Graphic analogues are supplied by the tremendous upward
thrust which appears so frequently in the paintings of Rubens—paintings of Christ bearing the cross, of the assump-

tion, and of Abraham's sacrifice, where the whole scene is viewed from underneath, so that the powerful figures swirl up into the sky. Wylie Sypher suggests that the concern of the Baroque artist with height and depth was a manifestation of triumph over the doubts and anxieties implied by the "frail, constrained hovering of mannerist forms," [14] and he argues that this motif was a natural outgrowth of the determination of the Council of Trent to inflame believers with a sense of otherworldliness. Actually this movement is inherent in many of the events recorded in the Gospel story—the flight of the angels down to earth and back to heaven, the uplifted eyes of the crowds at the Ascension, Christ's kneeling to wash the feet of the disciples:

Thus God lays everything aside, that He may serve His servants; heaven stoops to earth, and one abyss calls upon another, and the miseries of man, which were next to infinite, are excelled by a mercy equal to the immensity of God (II, 628–629).

The joys of Mary are pictured as joys meant for the whole world, resonating back and forth between Heaven and earth:

that the hopes of others may receive increase, that their faith may have confirmation, that their charity and eucharist may grow up to become excellent and great, and the praises of God may be sung aloud, till the sound strike at heaven, and join with the hallelujahs which the morning stars in their orbs pay to their great Creator (II, 58).

The motif of depth and height occurs again when Taylor compares the rewards of bearing the cross to "rich mines interred in the deeps and inaccessible retirements" (II, 392), and when he finds a valuable lesson in the retirement of the wise men upon their return from Bethlehem into "the recesses of religion and the delights of philosophy" (II, 87). And every time Taylor mentions humility, this movement is implied:

> When God descended to earth, He chose to be born in the suburbs and retirement of a small town, but He was pleased to die at Jerusalem, the metropolis of Judea; which chides our shame and pride, who are willing to publish our gaieties in piazzas and the corners of the streets of most populous places; but our defects, and the instruments of our humiliation, we carry into deserts, and cover with the night, and hide them under ground, thinking no secrecy dark enough to hide our shame, nor any theatre large enough to behold our pompous vanities; for so we make provisions for pride, and take great care to exclude humility (II, 66)

Another favorite motif of the Baroque artist, again with definite relevance to themes touched upon in the Gospels, is the contrast of light and darkness. A distinction which is often made in dealing with religious painting is that between the use of light for pleasing dramatic effects (Caravaggio's "Vocation of St. Matthew" will serve as an example of this technique) and its use as a genuinely analogical symbol, with the same depth of relevance that we have noted in Vaughan's use of the symbols of the journey and paradise. For three hundred years Rembrandt has been teaching the Western world what light can mean; Taylor also studied light carefully, and in *The Great Exemplar* he often makes effective use of what he learned. Unfortunately, many of his comparisons involving light can be dismissed as pretty or conventional: God and Christ are "the two great luminaries of heaven," and John the Baptist is compared to "the blushings springing from the windows of the east" (II, 164). But his references begin to get poignant when he talks about light seen through "transparent glass" or compares moments of inspiration to a flash of lightning that "makes the room bright, and our prayers end, and the lightning is gone, and we as dark as ever" (II, 129). Taylor saw in light a pulsating liveliness which reminded him of divine power; and in the way it endowed objects with richness, roundness, and fleshliness it was precisely the kind of material, nonabstract absolute his interpretation of Christ demanded.

One of Richard Crashaw's most grotesque images is his famous description of Mary Magdalen's eyes as "Two walking baths, two weeping fountains." Fountains are a common fixture, too, of emblem books, and there is plenty of flowing and overflowing, fullness and bursting in Taylor's prose. Rarely, though, are we invited to look beneath the surface of the images he creates, and this may indicate something of the superficiality of a good deal of Baroque art. Taylor's fountains are never manifestations of "the feminine principle" and rarely seem to suggest anything more than the most material forms of divine grace. Sometimes, though, with his flowing waters he does strike an emotional chord: he notes, for example, how God loves to nurture grace in the heart of the believer, and "if it takes root downwards, and springs out into the verdure of a leaf, He still waters it with the gentle rain of the holy Spirit" (II, 288). Taylor likens private devotions to "the petty drops of a water-pot" and public worship to rain from Heaven, and with a kind of Dantesque rapture he tells how God fills the hearts of believers "and the people sing *In convertando,* the song of joy for their redemption" (II, 160). Most pungent of all is, perhaps, the description of the overflowing joy of the shepherds—"as pre-

cious liquor, warmed and heightened by a flame, first crowns
the vessel, and then dances over its brim into the fire, increasing the cause of its own motion and extravagancy" (II,
84).

The paradox is a standard fixture of Baroque art—another
manifestation of the abundance reflected in welling tears and
overflowing fountains. Fletcher observes delightfully that
Christ made the world by speech before he learned to speak,
and held Heaven in his hands when He was being carried in
His mother's arms. It is the extravagance of the paradox that
links it to the Baroque spirit, the suggestion that truth is so
large, so manifold that it can be grasped only in terms of its
many opposites. Fletcher declares that he is celebrating, in
Christ's Victory and Triumph,

> The birth of Him that no beginning knew,
>   Yet gives beginning to all that are born;
> And how the Infinite far greater grew
> By growing less; and how the rising morn,
> That shot from heaven, did back to heaven return;
>   The obsequies of Him that could not die,
>   And death of life, end of eternity,
>   How worthily He died, that died unworthily.

Taylor's description of Christ's conversation with the woman
at the well is awash in paradoxes (the Biblical text, it might
be noted, is well stocked with ambiguities), and this rhetorical trick is used with great effectiveness in describing the
moments just before Christ was seized by the Jews:

The holy Jesus was born a tender and a crying infant; but is
adored by the *magi* as a king, by the angels as their God. He is

circumcised as a man; but a name is given Him to signify Him
to be the Saviour of the world. He flies into Egypt, like a distressed child, under the conduct of His helpless parents; but as
soon as He enters the country, the idols fall down, and confess
His true divinity. He is presented in the temple as the son of
man; but by Simeon and Anna He is celebrated with divine
praises for the Messias, the Son of God. He is baptized in Jordan
as a sinner; but the holy Ghost descending upon Him proclaimed
Him to be the well-beloved of God. He is hungry in the desert as
a man; but sustained His body without meat and drink for forty
days together by the power of His divinity: there He is tempted
of Satan as a weak man, and the angels of light minister unto
Him as their supreme Lord (II, 666).

Taylor sees Christ in terms of heights and depths, in terms
of light and darkness, in terms of fountains overflowing, in
terms of paradox, and finally in terms of the statuesque,
caught in stone like so many of the figures in paintings by
Veronese, with gestures determined by the demands of ritual,
not by any inherent vitality. Sypher calls this Baroque motif
"resolution in the flesh," and it would appear to be related
to a persistent tendency in Crashaw and to many sensuous
passages in Milton. Whether or not we accept Sypher's contention that its origin lies in the permission granted by the
Council of Trent for the use of images,[15] it makes a very definite contribution to the view of Christ which Taylor seems
to have been developing—a static figure, detached from time
and space, to be adored and celebrated, and who, by unhur-
ried movements, each one dedicated to the purposes of holiness, may inspire a similar pattern in men. C. S. Lewis's
observation that the purpose of ritual is to impose a patterned response upon the worshipper (it "hands over to the
power of wise custom the task . . . of being festive or sober,

gay or reverent, when we choose to be, and not at the bidding of chance" [16]) is underscored by a prayer from *The Great Exemplar,* in which just such a spirit is sought:

Give me a sober, diligent, and recollected spirit in my prayers, neither choked with cares, nor scatterd by levity, nor discomposed by passion, nor estranged from Thee by inadvertancy, but fixed fast to Thee by the indissoluble bands of a great love and a pregnant devotion: and let the beams of Thy holy Spirit descending from above enlighten and enkindle it with great fervours, and holy importunity, and unwearied industry (II, 483).

In intensely concrete images Christ is pictured as a pure figure newly stamped on the metal of religion and as tempering the mortar intended for the foundations of His church with blood and water. But always there is the feeling for the ordered, solemn grandeur of physical things, the high seriousness of monuments and pageants and all things that can be heard and seen and touched: Taylor pays reverence to Christ with "the lowest prostrations and humility of soul and body" (II, 70), and with marmoreal detachment he describes the bitter cup which every believer must drink—a "great antidote, which Himself, the great Physician of our souls, prescribed to all the world to cure their calamities" (II, 661).

Artistic faults—as well as intellectual ones—are inevitable in a book of this size, though Taylor generally avoids the Kitsch into which Baroque art all too easily falls.[17] Taylor is too eager to draw moral lessons from every act and word of Jesus, even when these lessons touch upon such pedestrian topics as the failings of the English clergy—a topic which persistently angers him but from which he cannot draw the fire that Milton did. Taylor's exquisite daintiness becomes silly prettiness when he describes the holy family as "full of poverty, and sanctity, and content" (II, 156) or calls Mary "a tender and pious parent" (II, 66). The description of the fourteen hundred bleeding infants is pure grotesquerie, and the questioning scribe is pompously called a "forward professor" (II, 332). Particularly annoying are Taylor's awkward Latin coinages, especially when they are paired with a really vivid image: fastuousness, subjicible, usufructuaries, respersion, intromission, abstersions, exinaniation, propassions, icterical, and extrinsecal. Words like these are perhaps the inevitable detritus of the kind of monumental enshrinement which Taylor was creating in *The Great Exemplar*.

What, in sum, did Taylor do with Christ, through whom, according to St. Paul, God was reconciling the world to Himself? In these pages·I have tried to suggest how Taylor resolved the issue by transferring it to the realm of art, where the central personality in the problem becomes part of a stone bas-relief or a quaint Dutch genre painting. The intellectual or theological side of the problem found expression in the Baroque qualities of grandeur and height, and the demands made upon Taylor for a personal experience of his savior were neutralized into warmth, light, pathos, and a sense of plenitude. Like the old Romans, Taylor appears to have seen religion as a civil institution, fundamentally and necessarily static, to be decked out in "exterior ornaments and accommodation" (II, 325) and to be cherished for its own intrinsic values. We should pray, Taylor suggests, that God fill our souls with religious feelings, "with impresses, dispositions, capacities, and aptnesses of religion" (II, 328). The faith which he found in the Anglican framework he judged to be perfect and complete, just as was the justification provided for each man at the moment of his baptism:

Never must we expect to be so again justified, and upon such
terms as formerly; the best days of our repentance are interrupted: not that God will never forgive them that sin after baptism, and recover by repentance; but that restitution by repentance after baptism is another thing than the first redemption.
. . . an imperfect, little, growing, uncertain, and hazardous reconciliation: a repentance that is always in production, a renovation by parts, a pardon that is revocable, a "salvation" to be
"wrought by fear and trembling" (II, 358).

To those who live in the dynamic, existentialist, post-
Kierkegaardian environment, in the world of *becoming,*
Taylor's stress on *being,* on obedience, order, piety, communion—qualities that every good man can exemplify, qualities far removed from the problems of Christ's self-awareness
or His historicity—will seem altogether too quiet, too detached, too classical. Indeed, his description of any believer's
last moments, which catches up all the somber exaltation of
Renaissance thinking about death, is entirely Stoic:

And after these preparatives, he may with piety and confidence
resign his soul into the hands of God, to be deposited in holy
receptacles till "the day of restitution of all things"; and in the
mean time, with a quiet spirit descend into that state which is
the lot of Caesars, and where all kings and emperors have laid
aside their glories (II, 700–701).

To some it may seem that this chapter has unduly neglected the power of the liberal tradition or has stressed too
heavily the place of the brain in religious matters. Neither

error has been intended; both have been made inevitable by the material. For that pattern of response which has been noted here—a tendency to sidestep vital issues—seems to run all through Taylor's career. He frequently puzzled his associates by his stand on theological issues; having advocated religious toleration, he drew back under pressure; a learned man, he is frequently careless about his facts and judgments; he seems to have participated in controversy with some hesitation, recognizing that he was essentially an aesthetic person; his treatment of death is oriented to stoic comfort rather than to a Christian faith in resurrection; and his treatment of moral and devotional problems is distinctly medieval. All of this put a man who lived in an intellectual and forward-looking age in an uncomfortable situation.

It may be, of course, that the very intellectual stresses with which we so frequently endow our religious problems have made these problems all the more unsolvable. If this is the case, then the aloofness which Taylor has created in *The Great Exemplar*—this distancing, this statuesque enshrinement—is less a neglect of issues than a way of living with them and a path to their solution, a solution not necessarily reached with the brain, but a solution nevertheless relevant to human needs.

Psyche's tasks— Milton's sense of self 6

No study of the 17th century humanist's discovery and organization of his powers could be brought to any kind of a significant close without some account of Milton's grandly sustained and many-leveled confrontation with his age. I have no intention, in this final chapter, of describing the achievement of Milton—an achievement for which the word "Miltonic" alone will suffice. Such a task, it seems to me, rests upon another considerably more germane to this study —the description of what might be called the "Miltonic stance," that sense of inner direction and inner resource which Milton developed as he formed the constantly shifting elements of his world into patterns that were meaningful to himself. There was not, actually, one stance but a whole series of stances, each blending with the others and all brought into harmony by some element which each reader identifies to suit himself. The isolation and description of the several worlds in which Milton lived has in recent years become a major task of Milton scholarship, and we have profited by specialized studies of his literary milieu, his response to "the Puritan dilemma," his interest in theology, his friendships and family relationships, and his contacts with the world of books and scholarship. His own conviction that a genuine humanist ought to be prepared to move in the most spacious and varied theatres is apparent in the broad curriculum which he lays out in the essay "Of Education" (1644) and in his determination that his charges will be prepared for nothing less than "all the offices, both private and public, of peace and war."

The stress in this essay upon personal achievement and personal maturity suggests that Milton was thoroughly grounded in the concept of *paideia,* that sense of the harmonious development of all the powers of the individual, that dedication to the noblest forms of achievement which characterizes the best of Greek humanistic thought. Indeed, it is conceivable that a reader who approached Milton with a good knowledge of personality theory but little information about the normal generalizations made by Milton scholars might conclude that here was another Goethe, a man who put his chief stress upon a thoroughly planned fostering of his own development, an infinitely careful organization of his world—a man for whom freedom was less a central issue than the climate essential for any real flowering of the personality.

The concern for maturity is a dominant note, too, in Milton's *Areopagitica* (1644), that most eloquent of pleas for an adult response to fresh ideas. And in no part of this essay does it sound more clearly than in Milton's allusion to the myth of Amor and Psyche. The essayist is considering what —if anything—should be done about heretical or subversive opinion. His proposal is to let the false and the true grow up together so that a normal attrition of the poorer ideas may occur naturally. Any separation of good and evil is difficult, Milton observes, since the two grow up so closely intertwined "that those confused seeds which were imposed on Psyche as an incessant labor to cull out and sort asunder, were not more intermixed." [1] But this problem and three others were solved for Psyche, and in each case the solution seems to have some relevance to the world of statecraft (Milton's immediate concern) and the problems of human development (his continuing interest).

Before these issues are considered, something must be said about the story of Psyche itself and its possible meanings. The best known account of the trials of Psyche is provided by Apuleius, in *The Golden Ass,* a romance-satire of the second century. It is told halfway through the fourth book by an old crone who has suffered deeply throughout her life. The old woman's tale of growth through suffering concerns a king and his three daughters. The beauty of the youngest arouses the jealousy of the two older girls and of Venus, who determines that Psyche is to be abandoned in an empty palace on a barren mountain. Venus's son Amor (Cupid or Eros in other versions) visits the lovely girl in the dark, but he forbids her to inquire about his identity. Psyche's curiosity is aroused pitilessly by her madly jealous sisters, so that one night, holding the lamp over her sleeping lover's head, she learns who he is but also awakens him with scalding drops of oil. For her disobedience she is condemned to wander, and while she wanders, to fulfill a number of tasks, any one of which, Venus hopes, will insure her rival's destruction. First Psyche must sort out a pile of scattered seeds, then pluck wool from the backs of fierce, man-eating sheep, fill a pitcher with water drawn from the Styx high up on a mountain, and finally visit Persephone in Hades, stopping to give help to no one on the way and returning with a box of beauty secrets, unopened. With the aid of certain natural forces Psyche completes all the tasks, failing only in one important detail: she opens the forbidden box to discover the secret of beauty. At this point, threatened by terrible punishment, she is rescued by Amor, spirited away to the palace of the gods, and there delivered of a child, Pleasure, the daughter of the God of Love.

What could this story, to which such brief reference is made in the *Areopagitica,* have meant to Milton? His interest in the old myth is suggested by references to it at both the beginning (*Comus*) and the end of his career (*Paradise Regained*). Just how much he saw in it is impossible to determine accurately, although this myth has been a fertile one: in Milton's day for painters, poets, and philosophers; in our day for students of anthropology, comparative religion, and the psychology of personality. In the Middle Ages the story of Amor and Psyche was among the most popular of all myths, since it lent itself well to allegorical reading. Fulgentius, in his *Mythographi Latini,* interprets the sisters as carnal desire, free will, and soul, but the tasks baffle him and he urges his reader to turn to Apuleius for help. Natalis Comes is of even less value, for although he comments in his

Mythologiae (1551) on the origins of Cupid, he says nothing about the boy's relations with Psyche. Edgar Wind points out that there was a long tradition in the Orphic cults of seeing in physical blindness the power of discerning spiritual beauty, so that Beroaldus (a commentator on Apuleius) can suggest that Cupid disappears when Psyche succumbs to the temptation of seeing him with her eyes. Pico and Ficino, according to Wind, are both aware of the painful cleansing that the lover must endure before "communion with the god." And there was also in the Renaissance a common tradition that the ordeals of Psyche were stages in mystical initiation —steps toward perfection.[2] These interpretations of the story, which link it with the insights of the pagan mystery cults into the nature of the human personality, make some of the 17th-Century versions appear very awkward indeed. Shakerley Marmion turns the story into light social comedy; Joseph Beaumont moralizes interminably upon it; Francis Bacon says that Cupid represents the force that draws the atoms to each other.

The myth does not seem to have been moored to its essential meanings again until the 20th Century, and then within a single year (1956) we had an important novel by C. S. Lewis on the growth of the personality through suffering (*Till We Have Faces*) and a study by the late Erich Neumann of the old myth as a Jungian archetype (*Amor and Psyche*).[3] Neumann sees in the story of Psyche an allegory of the development of the feminine consciousness from an elemental, preconscious state, in which all the factors of the later personality are indiscriminately mingled, to the final state of fully aware, adult identity and maturity. Caves, coffins, and the primitive symbol of the snake biting its own tail have all served as symbols of the dark chaos from which life came and to which it returns. The condition of Psyche as the youngest and most insignificant of three sisters, the darkness of the night in which Amor consummates his love, and the pile of seeds which Psyche must arrange—all are suggestive of this primal state. Abandoned in the mountain palace and perplexed as to the identity of her nightly visitor, Psyche encounters her first opportunity for growth and emergence. She may struggle against her plight, refusing to follow the command, or she may sense the intent of it and acquiesce. But even in this beautiful girl doubts and subconscious resentment cannot be suppressed completely: such at least is a possible interpretation of the shrill voices of her sisters who urge her to discover who the lover is. And from another viewpoint the advice is good, for this dark, subconscious state is more suggestive of some "blind servitude" to Venus, some preconscious state than of any fully mature self-awareness. So the sisters supply just the impetus needed to force the girl out of her darkness into full and authentic contact with the male. When the lamp shines upon the mysterious visitor, he is revealed not as a monster but (since Psyche is now becoming a mature woman) as a beautiful boy.

But drops of oil which fall from the lamp upon the boy scald him and force Venus to undertake the destruction of her rival. (Amor, too, is maturing, as he moves out of his mother's sphere of influence into a relationship with a woman whom he himself has chosen.) As she faces these dangers, Psyche is transformed into a kind of feminine Hercules, able to rescue not only the beautiful princess (herself) but the future hero as well.

How are the four "labors" which confront the young girl

to be interpreted? The question of the seeds to which Milton refers in the *Areopagitica* will be postponed briefly. Psyche's second task is to gather wool from shining golden sheep, fierce animals whose destructive powers fill the girl with dread. Neumann's suggestion is valuable; the sheep belong to the sun and embody the destructive powers normally associated with the male personality—rationality, keen analytic skill, physical strength, decisiveness of action. A reed by the brookside quietly provides Psyche with the needed counsel: the girl should be herself, relying on her own peculiarly feminine instincts, not attempting to overcome the sheep with trickery or force. Specifically, Psyche is to wait until evening, when the rams will be at rest and their wool can be plucked easily from the bushes. Patience will provide a far more fruitful contact than struggle.

Psyche's third task is to fill a crystal bowl with water drawn from the River Styx, as it rushes from the top of a mountain into a deep valley—an arc encompassing nothing less than Heaven, Earth, and Hell. The water, Neumann suggests plausibly, may be taken as a symbol of the vital, flowing energies of life—the power of the sun in a wholly formless state. To these tumbling, tumultuous forces Psyche must give form (hence the crystal bowl) without being shattered herself. Again, a being from the natural world—this time a strong-winged bird—provides the needed help.

With each victory Psyche's confidence develops until, in her fourth trial, she is able to face courageously a terrible journey into the regions of death to bring back to Venus a box containing Persephone's beauty secrets. In the course of this journey (which Lewis describes in a gripping manner), Psyche faces distractions of every variety—lures to turn this way and that, pitiful appeals to that sense of compassion which is part of the nature of every woman. And indeed she does finally succumb: having found the box after infinite hazards, she is unable to resist the temptation to open it. A deathsleep quickly overwhelms her but she is rescued by the intervention of Amor, who is now mature enough to stand up against his mother. Psyche's crime, it is argued, was natural and expected, it being the wish of every woman to be beautiful. The stability of Psyche as a person has been proven.

But it was the first task, sorting out the scattered seeds, that most powerfully caught Milton's imagination. Apuleius presumes the task to be impossible and pictures Psyche weeping bitterly over it. The situation as Lewis sees it is more hopeful: "In waking life a man would know the task impossible. The torment of the dream was that, there, it could conceivably be done. There was one chance in ten thousand of finishing the labour in time, and one in a hundred thousand of making no mistake." [4] Of the specific meaning of the seeds neither Neumann nor Apuleius has much to say. They seem to be cousins to the "specific seeds" or atoms described by Lucretius and to Nature's "germens" mentioned in both *King Lear* and *Macbeth*. These are the generative powers of Nature, *spermae* in Latin, *tejas* in Sanskrit. Speaking of the latter word, Abegg notes that it suggests not only generative power but sharpness, fire and heat, beauty or healthy appearance, energy, passion, and mental or magical strength.[5] In every case, a definite intensification of life is suggested. Surely also the sheer numerousness of the seeds has some significance, for it suggests that part of the challenge offered by human experience lies in the enormous va-

riety of things a man must face. I suspect that the problem
of the many as opposed to the one was prominent in Milton's
thinking when he wrote the *Areopagitica,* for most of the
mythical allusions in the essay are to stories in which numerousness is significant: the tales of "the fabulous dragon's
teeth," Typhon and Osiris, Proteus, and Janus. For Psyche
this is an awesome confrontation, but she is relieved of its
burden by ants (the natural instincts, perhaps), who bring
their tiny forms to bear effectively upon the heap of disorder.

It would seem, then, that the story of Psyche's tasks may
contribute much to our understanding of the emergence of
the personality through its involvement in the world. Maturity, it appears, is closely bound up with problems of
establishing order where there is chaos, discovering and employing skills and insights that are natural and personal,
giving form and structure to all the energies that stream
through the human personality, and developing a sure sense
of role—a measure of "ego-stability." The balance of this
essay will be devoted to pointing out some of the places in
Milton's poetry where these ideas occur. The product, I hope,
will be a statement about Milton's understanding of the
human personality and of the process of human development.

From his poetry we gather that Milton regarded the disorder of his several worlds as a major concern and felt that
the highest achievement to which he might aspire was ordering a segment of this chaos. The earliest important poem in
which disorder is a significant element is the Nativity Ode
(1629), where the moral confusion of the pagan world is
vividly presented—a world remarkable for the promiscuity
of its customs, beliefs, and objects of devotion. With the
coming of the Saviour, the disorder is intensified: oracles

grow "dumb," the "pale-ey'd Priest" is uninspired, the *"Lars and Lemures* moan with midnight plaint," the worshippers of "wounded Thammuz" mourn, "sullen *Moloch"* has abandoned his Idols, *Osiris* is fled, and it is in vain that Sorcerers worship "with Timbrel'd Anthems" dark. How seriously Milton took this destruction of an old order so that a new might arise is hard to say. By its very nature an ode celebrates the positive, the patterned, the obvious, and the ordered. And there can be little doubt of Milton's joy that with the coming of Christ a higher order has been found. This point is affirmed by the delightful image of the Shepherds "simply chatting in a rustic row," by the persistent references to music, and by the feeling of serenity that laps the entire scene:

> And all about the Courtly Stable,
> Bright-harness'd Angels sit in order servicable (243–244).

There is in *Comus* (1634) a much more compelling presentation of chaos in the impressive scene where the Sorcerer (leader of a "monstrous rout") tries to seduce the Lady with a wholly indiscriminate array of Nature's bounties—"cordial Julep," "fragrant Syrups," "soft delicacy" for her "dainty limbs," as well as Earth's "odors, fruits, and flocks," silk, and "precious gems." Here is a profusion of images that appeal to every sense, allusions to Greek mythology, to history, to philosophy; appeals to logic, to learning, to emotion, and even to practical morality! The "vermeil-tinctur'd lip," Comus argues, is not to be wasted at home:

> There was another meaning in these gifts,
> Think what, and be advis'd; you are but young yet (754–755).

Rarely has a young woman been met by such a congeries of rhetorical appeals, or responded so well. Her words mark the intellectual climax of the masque, and they seem to offer a vision of order based not on rapacious seizure of all that life holds forth but upon the exercise of restraint, temperance, and control. Her judgment, she affirms, will not be chained to her eyes:

> Imposter, do not charge most innocent nature,
> As if she would her children should be riotous
> With her abundance; she good cateress,
> Means her provision only to the good
> That live according to her sober laws
> And holy dictate of spare Temperance (762–767).

Her sense of order is too much for Comus; he shudders, fearing "Her words set off by some superior power," and although he attacks her, he is quickly routed by her brothers, a pair of gentle idealists too strong for the powers of Disorder.

The dominant impression left by *Samson Agonistes* (published 1671) is again that of a solitary figure wholly unable to deal with the multileveled chaos which confronts him. Within Samson rages a swarm of "restless thoughts." Slaves of Gaza surround him, and from his "pains and wrongs" there seems to be no escape. Moreover, he is tormented by the memory of older times when singlehanded he overcame vast armies—and by thoughts of a host of heroes of whom he has not been worthy. There arise thoughts, too, of that "peal of words" and "shameful garrulity" by which he was overcome. Before Samson, Dagon looms up as a symbol of vast, unfathomable confusion, and he resents having to perform in public when other entertainers are available:

> . . . Gymnic Artists, Wrestlers, Riders, Runners,
> Jugglers and Dancers, Antics, Mummers, Mimics (1324–1325)

The visits of Manoa and Dalila, with her "fair fallacious looks," further confuse him, for his wife makes a wide variety of appeals—to her husband's conjugal affection, his understanding of her weakness, her desire to help him and to have him for herself, and the power of the temptation which she faced. To the eventual structuring of all these elements Harapha, with his scorn for Samson's weakness, makes an important contribution. But the heart of the ordering process lies within Samson himself, specifically in his realization that the moment at which he stands offers some "important cause" into which he must project himself, that before him lies a perplexing but obviously pregnant situation which demands his faith, his heroic magnitude of mind, his God-granted sense of public duty. His ultimate success in bringing coherence into his confused world is indicated by the closing words of Manoa, who pleads that there be no lamenting, since

> . . . *Samson* hath quit himself
> Like *Samson,* and heroicly hath finish'd
> A life Heroic (1709–1710).

In *Paradise Lost* (to offer one more example) Milton presents a simply astonishing array of forms of disorder, at every level of human activity, with every conceivable significance. Stated in its most abstract form, the central theme of the poem is the release into the cosmos of a promiscuous, undifferentiated mass, with the subsequent adjustments undertaken by primal harmony. This theme is given concrete form in Book I, in terms of the revolt of Satan against God's

command. It is underscored by the most awesome actions—
Satan tumbles out of Heaven, is swallowed up by Hell, and
summons to his side an assembly of fantastically varied fol-
lowers. The great pedal note of confusion is picked up by the
ambiguity of Satan himself, by the complexity of the great
hall which the devils build, and by images of confusion
("whirlwinds of tempestuous fire"), monstrosity ("that Sea-
beast Leviathin"), and multitudinousness (the autumnal
leaves "that strow the brooks in Vallembrosa"). Book II,
which may be seen as an attempt to establish a false order
upon erroneous premises, closes with an impressive description of the chaos through which Satan must make his way
to Earth:

> . . . a dark
> Illimitable Ocean without bound,
> Without dimension, where length, breadth, and highth,
> And time and place are lost; where eldest *Night*
> And *Chaos*, Ancestors of Nature, hold
> Eternal Anarchy, amidst the noise
> Of endless wars, and by confusion stand.
> For hot, cold, moist, and dry, four Champions fierce
> Strive here for Maistry, and to Battle bring
> Thir embryon Atoms; they around the flag
> Of each his Faction, in thir several Clans,
> Light-arm'd or heavy, sharp, smooth, swift or slow,
> Swarm populous, unnumber'd as the Sands
> Of *Barca* or *Cyrene's* torrid soil,
> Levied to side with warring Winds, and poise
> Their lighter wings. To whom these most adhere,
> Hee rules a moment; *Chaos* Umpire sits,
> And by decision more imbroils the fray
> By which he Reigns: next him high Arbiter
> *Chance* governs all (II, 891–910).

In Book III, the plan for an ultimate divine order is presented; the description in Book IV of the garden offers an order as yet unchallenged and, therefore, of uncertain significance; in Book VI order and disorder confront each other directly; in Book X we learn of Eve's proposal that she and Adam have no children—a sterile order to be attained at the cost of life. The last books offer a dismal picture of the tragic pattern of human history, a pattern which is the ultimate result of Satan's—and Adam's—rejection of the divine pattern. But this may put the case too bluntly, for Adam, though he has rejected God's order, yet lives in an order of his own making, a contingent and tragic order, but an order nonetheless. Milton works out the differences between the two patterns in an infinitely touching way, revealing himself as one who reveres eternal order yet decides to choose a human pattern—sorry that a choice is required at all. Thus at the end he shows Adam accepting quite willingly a limited (but profoundly human) order—one based not on his desire to compete with God but on his willingness to submit:

> Henceforth I learn, that to obey is best,
> And love with fear the only God, to walk
> As in his presence, ever to observe
> His providence, and on him sole depend,
> Merciful over all his works . . . (XII, 561–565).

For Milton, then, disorder in all its variety was an important problem until the last. His contributions to a solution are always linked to human values, always involve choices conducive to the maturing of the human personality. A response to what the world offers made with restraint and temperance, acting in faith and according to one's own peculiar abilities,

retaining a sense of the complex forms of order beyond one's
own horizon—these were some of Milton's answers to this
important human problem.

The second of Psyche's tasks—plucking wool from the
man-eating sheep—seems to suggest that there is a subtle
power in the feminine way of looking at things that may
transcend the more obvious powers of the male. Neumann's
book, to which I have been referring, is directed at an explanation of the feminine personality, and my attempt to
apply his findings to Milton has met some criticism. Is not
Milton, it has been argued, the most masculine of poets? His
prose is dominated by images from the world of male struggle—"mettle . . . sinews . . . vigor." His last hero is a
wrestler. He seems to have promoted the image of himself as
a domineering controversialist, who could trade Latin insults
with Salmasius on better-than-even terms. And his personality is dominated by masculine traits—stability, certainty,
rationality, aggressiveness, activism. So Tillyard declares
that the tone of patience expressed in the sonnet, "When I
Consider," is very uncharacteristic of the poet. He finds it
again only in "Lycidas" and wonders if it is not perhaps a
sign of the exhaustion of vitality.

I note, on the other hand, widespread evidence throughout
Milton's poetry of a feminine response, of a kind much more
fundamental than Tillyard seems willing to recognize. Not
always, of course, does Milton speak approvingly of women,
and clearly he dislikes womanly men. The influence of Circe,
Eve, and Dalila is destructive; Samson vigorously condemns
his own "foul effeminacy"; and Adam has long since been
convicted of uxoriousness. But other figures like Urania

("the Heav'nly muse"), the Lady in *Comus,* and "my late espoused Saint," as well as certain persistent patterns of behavior seem to imply a sympathy with the feminine way of responding. We see a feminine buoyancy and adaptability in the shepherd lad in "Lycidas," who hitches up his cloak and moves off in search of new experiences and new challenges. I find a feminine element, too, in the willingness of many of Milton's characters to move forward in faith, even when the situation is not understood and the way is quite uncertain. With such faith Samson goes to the temple of Dagon, ignorant of what he will find there but confident that he will be guided to the proper response at the proper time. In much the same spirit the Christ of *Paradise Regained* moves out into the desert, his steps apparently wandering but actually

> . . . the Spirit leading,
> And his deep thoughts, the better to converse
> With solitude, till far from track of men,
> Thought following thought, and step by step led on,
> He enter'd now the bordering Desert wild . . . (I, 189–193).

Again, it might be said that the "feminine" personality depends more heavily upon intuition, upon one's feeling for a situation, than upon logic. This point is beautifully illustrated in the twenty-third book of Homer's *Odyssey,* when Penelope, exhausted by long years of disappointment and still not wholly convinced that this stranger is her husband, simply yields to Odysseus "in an act of intuitive faith." [6] And we see it in *Paradise Lost* when Adam, at the darkest moment of his short but already tragic life, clings unerringly

to his kind in a way that could not possibly find any rational
justification:

> Should God create another *Eve*, and I
> Another Rib afford, yet loss of thee
> Would never from my heart; no, no, I feel
> The Link of Nature draw me: Flesh of Flesh,
> Bone of my Bone thou art, and from thy State
> Mine never shall be parted, bliss or woe (IX, 911–916).

The feminine personality is marked, too, by strong faith in
the existence of a spiritual order, an order seen as responding
favorably or unfavorably to man, an order where gentleness,
love, and submission have their place. Such a faith seems to
underlie Milton's reflections upon his blindness in the sonnet
to Cyriack Skinner, the trust in virtue shown by the Lady in
Comus, and the sharp reply of Adam to Eve, when she
suggests (in a most masculine way!) that they might work
more efficiently in the garden if they divided up the task:

> . . . not so strictly hath our Lord impos'd
> Labor, as to debar us when we need
> Refreshment, whether food, or talk between,
> Food of the mind, or this sweet intercourse
> Of looks and smiles, for smiles from Reason flow,
> To brute deni'd, and are of Love the food,
> Love not the lowest end of human life.
> For not to irksome toil, but to delight
> He made us, and delight to Reason join'd (IX, 235–243).

To complete her second task, Psyche resorts to a power
more accessible to woman than to man—the power to relax
and let Nature operate in her own way. We have seen Browne

engaged in an essentially unsuccessful attempt to tap a closely related force. This is the power of which the Taoist is aware when he lets Nature function unimpeded. Hints of it have been found in *Oedipus Rex,* specifically in the view that a matriarchal society offers somewhat higher possibilities for human well-being than a society dominated by males. In our own century Martin Buber has talked about "an instinct to make contact" and "to establish relations." But in an age dominated by systems and rationalities—as the 17th century was—such an attitude had little chance to flower and the hints that Milton provides of his awareness of it have received little attention.

The meanings inherent in the third of Psyche's tasks—filling the slender crystal vase with water from the River Styx—seem to lie very near the heart of all Milton's creative activity. And the problem of raw or unharnessed energy so dominates Baroque aesthetics that evidently there is here a central concern of the whole age. What to do with popular rebellion against political and ecclesiastical tyranny, with conflicting moral systems, with the darker reaches of the human personality, with the whole vast struggle of the new to overcome the old—these issues rise when the meaning of this third task comes under discussion. Milton's strong interest in the problem of form is to be seen in his discussion in *The Reason of Church Government Urged Against Prelaty* (1642), of diffuse and brief epics and in his acceptance of the rules of Aristotle as "an enhancing of art." Of all the genres the epic must shape and control the greatest amount of highly diverse material. The generalities and abstractions by which a race lives must be made concrete and persuasive; broad social values must be endowed with personal meanings; the spiritual significance of physical struggles needs to be revealed; the way the past impinges on the present must be indicated. And these important issues must be imposed upon a rich canvas of wars fought, journeys made, cities destroyed, and civilizations founded. Such a challenge can be met only by an artist who sees form as the living, guiding basis of all creative effort.

But these energies of men do more than create important structural problems: they serve also as the content of works of art. Indeed, literature is full of the havoc wrought when human power or the power of a civilization escapes from control—Prometheus, Cassandra, Medea, young Attis in the Catullus poem all are its victims. Blake celebrates this elemental force in his enigmatic little poem about the tiger; Coleridge, through his tormented ancient mariner. The theme occurs in Milton as early as the Fifth Elegy (1629), as the poet describes his awareness of a new vigor that sweeps over him every year at the return of Spring:

Am I deluded? Or are my powers of song returning? And is my inspiration with me again by grace of the spring? By the spring's grace it is with me and—who would guess such a thing?—it is already clamoring for some employment. Castaly and the riven peak float before my eyes and by night I am beside Pirene in my dreams. My breast is aflame with the excitement of its mysterious impulse and I am driven on by the madness and the divine sounds within me. Apollo himself is approaching—I see the locks that are braided with Daphne's laurel—Apollo himself comes.[7]

A similar inner power is recognized by the Lady in *Comus,* who confidently assumes that it will put to naught all the rhetoric of the sorcerer:

> . . . the uncontrolled worth
> Of this pure cause would kindle my rapt spirits
> To such a flame of sacred vehemence,
> That dumb things would be mov'd to sympathize,
> And the brute Earth would lend her nerves, and shake,
> Till all thy magic structures rear'd so high,
> Were shatter'd into heaps o'er thy false head (793–799).

In *Samson Agonistes*, too, this theme is central—this theme of divinely bestowed energy dissipated, wasted, but finally regathered and put to use. Rather un-Greek is the stress which Milton puts on this theme. At the start of the drama Samson can do nothing but lament his "vast, unwieldy, burdensome" strength. He lies

> . . . at random, carelessly diffus'd,
> With languish't head unpropt,
> As one past hope, abandon'd,
> And by himself given over (118–121)—

as poignant a picture as could be imagined of great energy unformed and untapped. Each of the dialogues in which Samson participates contributes something to the reassembling of his power, and the climax of the poem comes with the messenger's description of the hero's last moments, when his strength was reintegrated:

> . . . with head a while inclin'd,
> And eyes fast fixt he stood, as one who pray'd,
> Or some great matter in his mind revolv'd.
> . . . straining all his nerves he bow'd;
> As with the force of winds and waters pent
> When Mountains tremble, those two massy Pillars
> With horrible convulsion to and fro
> He tugg'd, he shook, till down they came, and drew

The whole roof after them with burst of thunder
Upon the heads of all who sat beneath . . . (1636–1652).

The theme of formless energy suggested so vividly by the plunging waters of the River Styx sheds light, too, on one of the central figures of *Paradise Lost*. Satan has never been satisfactorily explained at the theological level because the attitudes he seems to embody are so hopelessly in conflict with the values usually associated with the rational, moral poet who hated him and yet felt his fascination. At another level (perhaps the "psychological") he becomes more plausible as the symbol of energy unformed, or deformed, and therefore tragically wasted. As the very essence of energized chaos he obviously cannot establish any relationship with the principle of Order, nor may he carry within himself any of the seeds from which order might come. Hence Milton's unremitting opposition to him at the conscious level—an opposition that goes even deeper than many undeniably vital theological issues. How powerful is the threat of this Satanic disorder can be gauged from the fact that nearly everything else in the poem is ranged in opposition and directed at the establishment of form and structure. Such is the function of the angelic hierarchy, the Creation of the world, the establishment of Nature (day and night, animals and their names, the garden), the creation of man and woman and the conjugal relationship, the establishment of a pattern of history. The poem itself is the crowning stroke which Milton, filled with the Renaissance idea of the planned life, gave to a tumultuous, energy-filled career.

The fourth of Psyche's tasks—the journey to Hell—is seen

by Neumann as a test of *ego stability,* of the power a maturing man develops to recognize the heart of his personality,
the fundamental direction of his life, and the peculiar distractions to which he is susceptible. The importance of this
theme in Western literature can be gauged by its persistence
in the epic tradition. For is not the most common of all epic
themes the journey in search of one's country, one's people,
one's own being? Milton's declaration, in the *Second Defense,*
"I will now mention who and whence I am," is merely the
boldest and most direct expression of an inner sense that can
be found in almost every line he wrote. This famous auto-
biographical passage, written in the face of attacks by Peter
du Moulin, reveals not only the strongest imaginable sense
of self-identity, but a lofty conception of this self (Milton
speaks proudly of his father as a man of "undeviating integrity"), a keen desire for self-enhancement (he made "a considerable progress in philosophy" before going to Cambridge), a strong sense of personal striving (from childhood
he was destined "to the pursuits of literature"), an element
of rationality ("I did not . . . run away into Italy, but of
my own accord retired to my father's house"), and a deep
longing to push out the bounds of his experience and his
engagement with the world ("I contracted an intimacy with
many persons of rank and learning").[8]

From the beautiful comment in *Manso,* "I believe that in
the dim shadows of night I too have heard the swans singing
on our river" (Nos etiam in nostro modulantes flumine
cygnos/ Credimus obscuras noctis sensisse per umbras) to
the despairing cry of Samson, "I to myself was false ere
thou to me," there is a constant celebration of the personality that comes to know itself and to value its own inner

consistency. In that impressive dialogue which makes up the central section of *Paradise Regained* (II, 298–IV, 393) Satan persistently holds up before Christ the challenge that He make something of Himself, that He forsake what appears to be a dubious and uncertain mission in order to create a startling impression on His age. Perhaps He may even engender some moral reforms!

> . . . With what ease,
> Endu'd with Regal Virtues as thou art,
> Appearing, and beginning noble deeds,
> Might'st thou expel this monster from his Throne
> Now made a sty, and in his place ascending
> A victor people free from servile yoke? (IV, 97–102)

But, as Christ indicates, for the man who knows himself thoroughly, there may be a higher commitment even than the commitment to moral reform. Satan's confusion, when this point strikes him, prompts his ugly question, "What dost thou in this World?" And the storm that breaks about Christ just after this incident may indicate that He has indeed been shaken by this challenge to His sense of personal mission. But with the morning, all anxieties end and the last temptation—that of the tower—is quickly and easily overcome. The last lines of the poem—

> . . . hee unobserv'd
> Home to his Mother's house private return'd—

offer a beautiful image of a man's recovery of the elemental bearings of his life.

Perhaps the most intense analysis in Milton's work of the struggle to maintain a sense of the self is to be found in

"Lycidas," a poem that depicts what I suppose is the first of the three or four central crises in Milton's life: in his early years came the threat (treated in this poem) to the loss of personality in death; his first marriage severely strained his concept of womanhood; his blindness forced upon him a reconsideration of his basic gifts, his mission, and his motives; and toward the end came the need (reflected in *Paradise Lost*) for a radical readjustment of his philosophy of man. No one can begin reading "Lycidas" without becoming aware that Edward King's death has aroused in Milton the very deepest anxieties—anxieties conveyed by aptly chosen words like "harsh . . . crude . . . pluck . . . forc'd . . . rude"); by the fear that Providence (the deities of sea and shore) has turned improvident; and by the thought that Nature has grown malignant (the canker kills the rose). A reference to the death of Orpheus implies that the wasting of young men is a repeated pattern in history. The famous passage, "What boots it with uncessant care," is perhaps the strongest challenge Milton ever permitted himself to voice against his sense of dedication, and the wistful suggestion that it might be better to "sport with Amaryllis" is virtually a momentary spiritual suicide—a decision to abandon the self so carefully constructed, so zealously guarded through the early years. Additional evidence that the good man is doomed to live in a thoroughly hostile world is provided by the bitter account of the corruption of that most honored of all offices—the ministry—and by the suggestion that King may have perished wholly without reason; the boat was cursed. The picture is complete; is it possible that a serious and earnest man's identity can be preserved? What possible significance is there to a lofty sense of dedication that passes over the lower goods of today for the uncertain, higher goods of tomorrow?

It is by a very complex process that Milton comes to reassert his faith in the importance of struggling toward a personality of one's own. Into it go his remembrance of the nature of true fame, his confidence that the moral order flaunted by a wicked clergy will reassert itself, a second look at the Spring landscape (the ground is purpled with "vernal flowers"), recollection of all the native English strength bound up in the protecting figure of St. Michael, and the very simple act of faith that "Lycidas is not dead." Each experience brings back to Milton's anxiety-ridden mind some important segment of his true self—his early dedication to God, his faith in a moral order and in the resurrection, his love of Nature, and his devotion to his country and its welfare. Milton's poetic journey through Hell ends with an image of a young man girding himself for activity, motivated by the recovery of his sense of purpose and direction: "Tomorrow to fresh Woods, and Pastures new."

The insights into the growth of the human personality bound up in the story of Amor and Psyche are certainly not peculiar to the 17th century—or to the 2nd century, when Apuleius wrote, or to the 20th century. They are applicable to any course of human development where potentially powerful personalities are faced with the task of ordering and synthesizing huge chunks of highly diverse materials and where there is a strongly felt challenge to create order where there is confusion (or more subtle forms of order in place of crude, inhuman ones), to act in a natural manner, to discover forms that will harness human energy, and to preserve and intensify one's identity in the face of the world's distracting challenges. Throughout this essay the problem of methodology has been consistently neglected. Whether Milton's reference to Psyche's task is an unthinking allusion or an indication of some really serious understanding of the myth; how acceptable (in the light of widespread scepticism over Jungian philosophy) is Neumann's reading of the myth; the possibility (and wisdom) of attempting to reduce Milton's thinking to a series of abstract propositions—these are fascinating problems, but they lead away from the central issues of this chapter and of this book. I have tried to suggest here that the insights which some modern students have found in the old myth parallel some of the most important motifs in Milton's poetry. If these are meanings of which Milton was not entirely consciously aware, they are nonetheless meanings highly suggestive for a reading of his poetry and for a study of the way he organized his world.

Conclusion

Through an examination of half a dozen English writers of the 17th Century, I have tried in these pages to suggest some of the ways that men who lived in a very rich and stimulating age tried to shape the events that were most meaningful to them into general patterns of response. The variety of events which these writers faced is an always-impressive reflection of the breadth and complexity of the world in which they lived. Issues were developing in the explosive manner which we have come to associate with our own century. New facts impinged upon men with a sometimes terrifying force, relentlessly demanding some kind of response. Many of these facts were no doubt revolutionary in themselves, but the impact of the sheer volume of fresh material must not be underestimated: the only sight in a library more impressive than a full set of the Proceedings of the Royal Society is a full set of the Library of Anglo-Catholic Theology! William Petty left fifty-three chests of papers and fifty separate volumes. Bacon and Burton offer long lists of questions for which they want answers. John Milton's contacts with his world—as they are recorded in Professor French's *Life Records*—are astonishing in number and variety. And in this book I have attempted to suggest how widely the interests of John Evelyn ranged, how much peculiar knowledge Browne had collected, how Burton constantly expanded his book as his insights deepened.

Paralleling this intense concern with the objective world there is, in what I see of the 17th Century, a growing recognition of the importance of subjective and personal factors in the developing experience of man. This is the great century of the "character" genre, of the humor plays, and of the philosopher-psychologists—Hobbes, Descartes, Bacon, and Spinoza. At the beginning of the century John Donne is making poetry out of very private erotic experiences and then later turning the experience of sickness into deeply meaningful prose. Near the end of the century Thomas Sprat surveys the philosophical potential of his fellow Englishmen and concludes that

they have commonly an unaffected sincerity; that they love to deliver their minds with a sound simplicity; that they have the middle qualities, between the reserv'd subtle southern, and the rough unhewn Northern people: that they are not extremely prone to speak: that they are more concern'd, what others will think of the strength, than of the fineness of what they say: and that an universal modesty possesses them.[1]

We have seen this inward movement in Browne's attempt to turn even the most objective scientific facts into instruments of ecstasy; in Taylor's transfer of ethical, theological, and Biblical data over to the aesthetic and subjective realms; in Milton's constant distillation of personal experience into poetry; and in the very intimate concerns about which Burton writes. The significance of this cultural development, this enriching of one part of human experience, has been well described by John Dewey:

The modern discovery of inner experience, of a realm of purely personal events that are always at the individual's command, and that are his exclusively as well as inexpensively for refuge, consolation and thrill is also a great and liberating discovery. It implies a new worth and sense of dignity in human individuality, a sense that an individual is not a mere property of nature, set in a place according to a scheme independent of him, as an article is put in its place in a cabinet, but that he adds something, that he makes a contribution.[2]

Through the interaction of these two worlds—the big world and the small, the outer world and the inner—new forms of personal power seem to have emerged. In the titles of Renaissance books which survey broad fields, the word "theatre" (from the Greek θεάομαι, to see) appears frequently and seems to suggest a new quality of vision, a new firmness and confidence of manner based on new and direct contact with "the world out there." Milton's dream of those Satanic "thoughts that wander through eternity" captures this sense of power. Donne, bound to the close prison of his sickbed, found his thoughts outstripping the sun: "Our creatures," he writes, "are our thoughts, creatures that are born giants; that reach from east to west, from earth to heaven; that do not only bestride all the sea and land, but span the sun and firmament at once; my thoughts reach all, comprehend all." [3] The force of what Bacon had to say about the possibilities of science came not from his scientific knowledge, which was limited and inaccurate, but from the tremendous personal enthusiasm which he projected to others. A similar kind of personal involvement gives force to Evelyn's writings on forestry, to Browne's efforts to penetrate into realms of being normally shut off from man, and to Milton's treatment of divorce laws, the history of the regulation of printing, and the theory of education.

About the bare, basic facts that go to make up a man's experience no value judgments are possible. This point was made by David Hume, who, at the beginning of the 18th century, raised questions about the kind of mind that would carry a man along most effectively, about whether a clear head or a quick and penetrating apprehension, a sure or a ready judgment was the most valuable mental trait. " 'Tis evident," he concluded, "we can answer none of these questions, without considering which of these qualities capacitates a man best for the world, and carries him farthest in his undertakings." [4] Hume was certainly right, and he directs us to the key issue. For there is validity in asking about the context in which certain mental qualities and certain external events have appeared, the way in which they have been combined, the use to which they have been put. This interplay of inner and outer worlds is a process determined by man's creativity, his ability to improvise, his power to see similarities and differences, to adjust breadth of vision to understanding of detail, to think about himself and to forget himself, to keep in mind always certain basic sources of meaning. I have tried in this book to estimate my subjects in these terms.

Notes

JOHN EVELYN   Chapter 1

1 John Evelyn, *Miscellaneous Writings,* ed. William Upcott (London, 1825), p. 545.
2 See especially Norman Brett-James, *The Growth of Stuart London* (London, 1935). In fifty years of the 17th century, London doubled its area and population, reaching its limits of growth within the walls. For some time the city refused to accept new subdivisions outside the walls, and there was talk of creating a rival city *extra mura.* Then, as now, suburbs were thought to contribute to the ruin of a city. Elizabeth, James I, Charles I, and Cromwell all tried to stem the growth but failed. Besides breeding plague, oversized cities were regarded as a threat to the monarchy. Population estimates vary widely: Creighton estimates 224,275 in 1605 for greater London. James Howell set the figure for 1657 at one and a half million, while in 1665 the French ambassador estimated only 600,000. Both of these latter figures Brett-James thinks too high: one-half million before the plague and 400,000 after it are the figures he provides. A reliable estimate puts the population in 1700 at 674,350. The region of greatest growth was the west

end (since prevailing winds blew away the odors from factories located on the other side of the city). An influx of workers and commercial people brought growth in the east.

3 John Evelyn, *Diary and Private Correspondence* (London, 1887), III, 295. All quotations from the letters come from this edition.

4 For many carefully documented examples of Evelyn's borrowings see the six-volume edition of his *Diary*, edited by E. S. DeBeer (Oxford, 1955). All future references to the Diary are to this edition.

5 *Sylva, or a Discourse of Forest-Trees and the Propagation of Timber* (London, 1664), p. 2.

6 *Ibid.*, p. 7 ("Of the Seminary").

7 For a description of this garden see W. G. Hiscock, *John Evelyn and His Family Circle* (London, 1955), pp. 28 ff.

8 B. Sprague Allen, *Tides and English Taste, 1619–1800* (New York, 1958), I, 114–163.

9 Evelyn also translated a book by Nicholas Bonnefons, *Le Jardinier François,* in which he refers to a larger work of his own on parterres, grottoes, and groves. This is the elaborately conceived but never completed *Elysium Britannicum,* a book which Evelyn was always expanding, but never found satisfactory. In the preface to the Bonnefons translation he proudly describes soil dressing, the growing of wall plants, and pruning as "a peculiar science not to be attained amongst Cabbage Planters." Another original book, very popular in his day, was Evelyn's little *Kalendarium Hortense,* or *Gardener's Almanac,* which offered a list of tasks to be performed each month of the year in the garden.

10 Evelyn's proposal came to naught. There was an inquiry in 1718, but authorities admitted they could not cope with the problem.

11 *The Growth of Stuart London*, p. 193.

12 J. L. and Barbara Hammond, *The Rise of Modern Industry,* fifth edition, revised (New York, 1937). See especially Part 2, pp. 66–189.

13 Abraham Wolf, *A History of Science, Technology, and Philosophy in the 16th and 17th Centuries* (London, 1950), p. 553.

14 *Technics and Civilization* (New York, 1934), pp. 110, 119.

15 *Miscellaneous Writings*, p. 529.

16 Cf. *Diary,* III, 333, where Evelyn describes going to "consult about the new modeld-ship at *Lambeth,* the intention being to reduce that art to as certaine a Method as any other part of *Architecture.*"

17 See *Diary,* III, 495, and *Letters,* III, 198 (to Henry Hammond, 4 August 1667): "I know your honor cannot but have thoughts and resolutions of repairing and collecting them together one day; but there are in the mean time certain broken inscriptions, now almost obliterated with age and the ill effects of weather, which will in a short time utterly be lost and perish, unless they be speedily removed to a more benign and less corrosive air."

18 For a new translation see the edition prepared by Archer Taylor (Berkeley, 1950). If Evelyn's concern marks the beginning of a new age in bibliographic science, the mid-20th Century has seen still further

revolutions. At least one great European university now offers a Ph.D. in bibliography.

19 The Arundel collection is thought to have included over five hundred manuscripts and about four thousand printed books. See *Diary*, IV, 144.

20 *Sculptura*, ed. C. F. Bell (London, 1906), p. 138.

21 A frequently suggested date for this book—1651—would push this interest back even further.

22 See W. G. Bell, *The Great Fire of London in 1666* (London, 1951), pp. 230 ff., for reprints of plans.

23 Readers of Dickens' *Our Mutual Friend* will remember the "minding schools" set up for the care of orphans and illegitimate children, as well as the terror of the saintly Betty Higden that the children under her care might be taken to the poorhouse by the state. Evidently something of the system to which Evelyn refers was still in effect in the 19th Century.

24 *London Revived*, ed. E. S. DeBeer (Oxford, 1938), p. 54.

25 J. U. Nef in *Cultural Foundations of Industrial Revolution* (Harper Torchbooks: New York, 1960) describes (chapter six) many of the refinements—like fine glass and playing cards—that began to appear after the Civil War.

26 See Bell, *The Great Fire*, p. 133.

27 *An Account of Architects and Architecture* (1697), in *Miscellaneous Writings*, p. 367.

28 A. O. Lovejoy, *Essays in the History of Ideas* (Capricorn Books: New York, 1960), pp. 137–138.

29 See DeBeer's discussion of architectural terms, *Diary*, VI, 1–7.

30 For a more sympathetic account of Creech's death see Voltaire, *Philosophical Letters*, "Miscellany," ed. Ben Ray Redman (The Viking Portable Voltaire: New York, 1962), p. 220.

31 *Science and the Modern World* (New York, 1926), pp. 282–283.

32 Rollo May, *Existence* (New York, 1958), p. 19.

ROBERT BURTON   Chapter 2

1 Edward Reynolds, *A Treatise of the Passions and Faculties of the Soule of Man* (London, 1640), Chapter 37.

2 *The Anatomy of Melancholy* (London, 1621), p. 8. Unless otherwise noted, references are to this, the first edition. Both Preface and Partition One begin with page one.

3 *The Anatomy of Melancholy*, ed. A. R. Shilleto (London, 1912–1913), I, 15. This edition, in three volumes, incorporates material added after the first edition. It is used where quotation from the first edition is not crucial to the argument.

4 *Don Quixote*, translated by P. Motteaux (Everyman's Library: London, 1906), II, 144.

5 See *The Psychiatry of Robert Burton* (New York, 1944), p. 19; *Sanity in Bedlam* (East Lansing, Michigan, 1959), p. 38; *Character and Social Structure* (New York, 1953), p. 123.

6 In discussing Schopenhauer, Edward Hitschmann has described the mechanism of resentment, pointing out that a person who has been "disappointed and dejected by lack of success, lack of recognition and feelings of imperfection" may repress his feelings into his unconscious, apparently because his capacity for giving vent to them in any stronger fashion has already been destroyed, giving way to a sense of powerlessness. As old values are seen to be false, a new set of values is adopted. In the course of this change, the outlook on the world is distorted. See *Great Men: Psychoanalytic Studies* (New York, 1956), p. 94.

7 See *Sanity in Bedlam* and *Bibliographia Burtoniana* (Stanford, 1931).

8 See Witherspoon and Warnke, *Seventeenth-Century Prose and Poetry* (New York, 1963), p. 645.

9 A recent and informative study of the university curriculum in 17th century England is William Costello's *The Scholastic Curriculum at Early 17th-Century Cambridge* (Cambridge, Mass., 1958). Physics, "the science of the changeable," was a vast conglomeration of things—the study of body or substance, the organization of the cosmos, the problem of knowledge and the senses, animation, psychology, and the problem of creation. The situation was much the same at Oxford. In neither university would there have been anything to challenge a student interested in the more subtle aspects of medicine.

10 Shilleto, II, 221.

11 *Sanity in Bedlam*, p. 28.

12 And see Shilleto, I, 31.

13 Shilleto, III, 9.

14 Shilleto, III, 59, 61.

15 Shilleto, III, 251-2.

16 *Heaven upon Earth and Characters of Vertues and Vices,* ed. R. Kirk (New Brunswick, 1948), p. 185.

17 *Sanity in Bedlam*, p. 52.

18 *The Praise of Folly* (Princeton, 1941), pp. xiv ff.

19 *Don Quixote*, I, 158.

20 *The Anatomy of Robert Burton's England* (Berkeley, 1952), p. 27.

21 *Sanity in Bedlam*, p. 14.

22 Quintilian, *Institutia Oratoria* (Loeb Classical Library: London, 1921), II, 59.

23 *Tristram Shandy*, ed. James Work (New York, 1940), p. 73.

24 See Mueller, *The Anatomy of Robert Burton's England,* Chapter 4.

25 This view is supported by Babb, *Sanity in Bedlam,* p. 15.

26 Of the two references in Shilleto's edition of the *Anatomy* (Preface) to Laurentius, that on page 32 is not in the first edition; that on page 138 is, but it occurs on page 70, at the very beginning of the section I have argued is late.

27 A good idea of the relative decline of the importance of the humoral theory can be had from an examination of the materials presented by Hunter and MacAlpine in *Three Hundred Years of Psychiatry* (London, 1963).

SIR THOMAS BROWNE   Chapter 3

1 *The Diary and Correspondence of John Evelyn, F. R. S.,* ed. William Bray (London, 1887), III, 109.
2 *The Great Exemplar, The Whole Works of the Right Reverend Jeremy Taylor, D.D.,* ed. C. P. Eden (London, 1847–54), II, 134.
3 *John Milton, Complete Poems and Major Prose,* ed. M. Y. Hughes (New York, 1957), p. 727.
4 See Frank Barron, "Diffusion, Integration, and Enduring Attention" in *The Study of Lives,* ed. R. W. White (New York, 1963), pp. 244, 245.
5 See R. H. Blyth, *Zen in English Literature* (Tokyo, 1942).
6 *Zen Flesh, Zen Bones: A Collection of Zen and Pre-Zen Writings,* compiled by Paul Reps (Tokyo, 1957), p. 123.
7 A. H. Watts, *The Way of Zen* (New York, 1957), p. 194.
8 D. T. Suzuki, *Zen Buddhism* (Doubleday Anchor Books: New York, 1956), p. 256.
9 Harold G. Henderson, *An Introduction to Haiku* (Doubleday Anchor Books: New York, 1958), p. 18.
10 In his *Treatise of the Passions* (1640), Edward Reynolds, an Anglican clergyman, declares that education, custom, faith and culture of the mind all can lessen the soul's dependence on the body and produce "those *Raptures* and *Ecstasies* which raise and ravish the Soul" (p. 10), and among the passions he lists the "mental passions" or *Apex Animae* which the schoolmen call "Ecstasie or Rapture." The Cartesian philosopher and Royalist statesman, Sir Kenelm Digby, closes his treatise, *The Nature of Mans Soule* (1645), with an ecstatic description of his bliss at the thought of immortality: "Which way soever I looke, I loose my sight, in seeing an infinity round about me. Length without points. Breadth without lines. Depth without any surface. All content, all pleasure, all restlesse rest, all an unquietnesse and transport of delight, all an extasie of fruition" (p. 30). And Meric Casaubon argues, in his *Treatise Concerning Enthusiasm* (1655), that the various ecstatic states —divine, poetic, philosophical, and rhetorical—all have perfectly predictable natural causes and are not to be attributed to divine inspiration or diabolic possession. Nevertheless, he clearly grants that such states can exist, testifies that reading Plato is his best inspiration, and wonders if they can be self-induced.
11 See Margaret Wiley, *The Subtle Knot: Creative Scepticism in Seventeenth-Century England* (Cambridge, 1952), pp. 137, 138, 146; E. S. Merton, *Science and Imagination in Sir Thomas Browne* (New York, 1949), p. 18; and W. P. Dunn, *Sir Thomas Browne: A Study in Religious Philosophy* (Minneapolis, 1950), p. 15.
12 *The Meeting of East and West* (New York, 1946), pp. 406–410. Browne's response to ideas suggests a passage from Santayana's *Persons and Places:* "I loved speculation for itself, as I loved poetry, not out of worldly respect or anxiety lest I should be mistaken, but for the

splendor of it, like the splendor of the sea and the stars" (New York, 1944), p. 250.

13 *The Works of Sir Thomas Browne,* ed. Simon Wilkin (London, 1852), II, 321.

14 Charles Luk, *Ch'an and Zen Teaching:* First Series (London, 1960), pp. 11–12.

15 Suzuki, *op. cit.,* p. 142.

16 Roger Godel, "The Contemporary Sciences and the Liberative Experience of Yoga," in *Forms and Techniques of Altruistic and Spiritual Growth,* ed. P. A. Sorokin (Boston, 1954), p. 8.

17 Anthony Bloom, "Yoga and Christian Spiritual Techniques," in Sorokin, *op. cit.,* p. 94.

18 G. Rowley, "Composition," in *Principles of Chinese Painting* (Princeton, 1959).

19 *Modes of Thought* (New York, 1938), p. 65.

20 *Milton and Forbidden Knowledge* (New York, 1955), p. 64. On the meaning of circles see the essay by Emerson and the article by Frank Huntley, *Journal of the History of Ideas,* XIX (June, 1953), 353–364. I am not convinced by Huntley's argument that because the metaphor of the circle runs through Browne's religious thought and his astronomical speculations, Browne felt or perceived organic correspondences between the two realms. In his recent book on Browne, Huntley argues that Browne joined the two worlds by metaphor. I do not know what this means.

21 See E. Neumann, "The Creation Myth," in *The Origins and History of Consciousness* (New York, 1954).

22 *Science and the Modern World* (New York, 1926), pp. 41–42.

23 Quoted from manuscript by Dunn, *op. cit.,* pp. 157–158.

24 See Dunn, *op. cit.,* pp. 42, 43, 119.

25 Germaine Brée, in discussing the aesthetic theory of Camus, observes that the gratuitousness of the creative artist's work is "a perpetual challenge to his consciousness; it is 'a unique chance to keep his consciousness alert and to fix its adventures.' His task requires strict discipline, the will never to yield a fragment of his lucidity. The artist stands, therefore, fully armed in the face of the universe, refusing the somnolence it offers" (*Camus,* New Brunswick, 1959, p. 243).

26 See Anthony Bloom, *op. cit.,* p. 102. Whitehead observes that *importance* arises from a fusion of finite and infinite: "The mystic, ineffective slumber expresses the vacuity of the merely infinite" (*Modes of Thought,* p. 108).

27 *The Phenomenon of Man* (Harper Torchbooks: New York, 1961), p. 78.

HENRY VAUGHAN   Chapter 4

1 *Henry Vaughan: Experience and the Tradition* (Chicago, 1959), Chapter I, Chapter IV, p. 92.

2 Page 509. All page references are to *Works,* ed. L. C. Martin, 2nd edition (Oxford, 1957).

3 Gordon Allport, *Becoming: Basic Considerations for a Psychology of Personality* (New Haven, 1960), p. 77.
4 *Poetry and Dogma* (New Brunswick, 1954).
5 *A History of Modern Wales* (London, 1950).
6 *The Welsh People* (London, 1902), p. 456.
7 E. C. Pettet, *Of Paradise and Light* (Cambridge, 1960), p. 19.
8 "Kafka's Quest," in *The Kafka Problem* (New York, 1946), pp. 47–62.
9 *The Rise of Puritanism* (New York, 1938), p. 142.
10 *Middle-Class Culture in Elizabethan England* (Chapel Hill, 1935), p. 279.
11 *The Divine Comedy* (The Modern Library: New York, 1950), p. 238.
12 *Archetypal Patterns in Poetry* (London, 1951), pp. 110–113.
13 In *Myth and Myth-Making*, ed. Henry Murray (New York, 1960), p. 62.
14 *Ibid.*, p. 73.
15 *Henry Vaughan: A Life and Interpretation* (Oxford, 1947), p. 162.

JEREMY TAYLOR   Chapter 5

1 *The Whole Works of the Right Reverend Jeremy Taylor*, ed. C. P. Eden (London, 1847–54), V, 369.
2 "Notes on Taylor," *The Literary Remains of Samuel Taylor Coleridge* (London, 1836), p. 331.
3 Quoted by C. J. Stranks, "Jeremy Taylor," *The Church Quarterly Review* CXXXI (1940–41), 31–63.
4 Heinrich Wölfflin, *Principles of Art History* (Dover Publications), pp. 73 ff., 124 ff.
5 *Anglicanism*, ed. P. E. More and F. L. Cross (London, 1951), p. xxxiii.
6 Some evidence of the popularity of books like these is to be seen in the fact that Dent's book went through twenty-five editions before 1640, while Bayly's saw thirty-six before 1636.
7 See Charles C. Butterworth, *English Primers* (Philadelphia, 1953).
8 *The Vita Christi of Ludolphus, the Carathusian*, ed. Sister Mary Bodenstadt (Washington, 1944), p. v.
9 Sebastian de Grazia (*Of Time, Work, and Leisure,* New York, 1962) observes, "If you have a problem, you are no longer objective. Your autarchy, your capacity to be your own company, is gone. Knowledge now has to pertain to the problem. You cannot contemplate, you can only intently observe the problem you are slicing" (p. 420). I have suggested that Browne suffered from a similar indisposition.
10 *Introduction to the Literature of Europe* (New York, 1864), II, 52.
11 A useful discussion of "Baroque," as it applies to both the fine arts and literature, is to be found in Sypher's *Four Stages of Renaissance Style* (Anchor Books: Garden City, New York), pp. 180 ff. Wölfflin is a better authority but his presentation is not so closely geared to literature.
12 Adolf Harnack, *What Is Christianity?* (New York, 1906), p. 30.
13 *The Place of Jesus Christ in Modern Christianity* (New York, 1929), p. 101.
14 Sypher, *op. cit.,* p. 234.
15 *Ibid.*, p. 187.

16 *A Preface to Paradise Lost* (London, 1942), p. 21.
17 Albert Guerard, *A Preface to World Literature* (New York, 1940), pp. 102 ff.

JOHN MILTON   Chapter 6

1 John Milton: *Complete Poems and Major Prose,* ed. M. Y. Hughes (New York, 1957), p. 728.
2 Edgar Wind, *Pagan Mysteries in the Renaissance* (New Haven, 1958), Chapter Ten.
3 *Amor and Psyche* was originally published in 1952. Many of the ideas presented in this book are more fully developed in *The Great Mother* (New York, 1955) and *Origins and History of Consciousness* (New York, 1954).
4 C. S. Lewis, *Till We Have Faces* (New York, 1956), p. 256.
5 C. G. Jung, *Psychology of the Unconscious* (London, 1919), p. 101.
6 W. B. Stanford, *The Ulysses Theme: A Study in the Adaptability of a Traditional Hero* (Oxford, 1963), p. 59.
7 Hughes, p. 38.
8 Hughes, pp. 828–829; and see Gordon Allport, *Pattern and Growth in Personality* (New York, 1961), pp. 127 ff.

CONCLUSION

1 Thomas Sprat, *History of the Royal Society,* ed. Jackson Cope and H. W. Jones (St. Louis, 1958), p. 114.
2 *Experience and Nature* (La Salle, Illinois, 1958), p. 143.
3 *Devotions upon Emergent Occasions* (Ann Arbor Paperbacks, 1959), p. 23.
4 *Philosophical Writings* (Edinburgh, 1826), II, 403.

Index